To PASTO

Thanks for A
wonderful, spiRitual
weekend.

1-20-02
NESDA

A Touch of Reality:

An In the Box Process for Out of the Box Thinking

By Robert D. Johnson

Oakhill Press

Greensboro, North Carolina

This publication is designed to provide accurate and authoritative information in regard to the subject matter covered. It is sold with the understanding that the publisher is not engaged in rendering legal, accounting, or other professional service. If legal advice or other expert assistance is required, the services of a competent professional person should be sought. *From a Declaration of Principles jointly adopted by a committee of the American Bar Association and a committee of Publishers.*

10 9 8 7 6 5 4 3 2 1

Johnson, Robert D., 1950–
    A touch of reality: an in the box process for out of the box thinking / by Robert D. Johnson.
        p.   cm.
    Includes bibliographical references and index.
    ISBN 1-886939-23-3 (hardbound)
    1. Teams in the workplace.   I. Title.
    HD66.J653   1998
    658.4 ' 036 -- dc21   97-29376

Library of Congress Cataloging in Publication Data

Oakhill Press
3400 Willow Grove Court
Greensboro, NC 27410-8600
Printed in the United States of America

Contents

Foreword

Two years ago Bob Johnson introduced the Bcube"! process to our team at GKA. Having spent almost two decades of my life with system thinking and system dynamics, I was already enthusiastic about the value of helping teams surface, explore, and restructure mental models. Also as founder of GKA, I felt confident that our team would get value out of going through the Bcube"! process even though they were highly experienced at working with other teams. My primary concerns prior to the process were that our team might resist on the basis that their expertise in systems thinking and that the personal additional value I would gain might be limited as I had already seen the box in action and heard Bob's debrief.

When I actually sat down with my team inside the Bcube"! process, I was astounded at the intensity of the experience. Talking about experiential learning, or even facilitating for others is completely different from experiencing it with your own team. We all learned new and important things about each others ways of thinking and behaviors. This was surprising to me because many of us had worked together for years. We had so much fun we were able to create a safer atmosphere for talking about some of our deeper more difficult issues. One fascinating aspect of the process was that in playing the game our team replicated many of the behaviors on a micro scale that we were having over a longer time frame in our real work. But in the game, which had a content focus totally unrelated to the content of our actual work, we were able to separately address the behaviors apart from the content issues. Also, when we sat down together for the game exercises we were all equal, there was no knowledge advantage between the professional staff and others. I am repeatedly amazed at the wide range of insights that a team can generate from what appears to be a very simple experience. Don't let its simplicity fool you. It is a powerful vehicle for exposing and discussing team dynamics.

Since the publication of Peter Senge's book *The Fifth Discipline: The Art and Practice of the Learning Organization* many organizations and teams are discovering how challenging the implementation of the five disciplines can be. The Bcube"! process is a powerful intervention for exploring and experiencing these concepts of mental models, team learning, and shared vision and gives these teams a powerful new approach that can be used at any level in an organization. This process can provide a tangible, real life experience that can be a foundation for introducing any of the five disciplines separately or together.

Over the last decade and a half of working closely with organizations implementing systems thinking and system dynamics approaches I have encountered many "soft-system" issues generation techniques developed to help team surface mental models and assumptions. In FASTbreak"!, for example, I often use the emergent agenda variation of the hexagon technique. We ask a team the question what are the most important issues for this team to discuss for us to succeed in our mission? We also ask for strong opinions, emotions, etc. We ask each person to articulate their ideas in a few sentences and then translate them into a couple of words on six inch hexagon shaped magnetic disks or post-it notes. Using extensions of De Bono's color coding scheme we are able to quickly surface and explore team mental models. I always felt the color coding and alternative role playing were important ways to make it safer and easier for people to express emotion and go beyond the cognitive filters present in many verbally based brainstorming tools. In the Bcube"! process I often sense that many participants are even more able to surface, express, and perceive issues in their behaviors and interactions that they are not able to articulate and may not even be conscious of. Combining the Bcube"! process with other processes from the five disciplines may yield exciting innovations and breakthroughs in our ability to facilitate team learning.

If your teams are trying to get out of the box thinking I strongly recommend that you use the Bcube"! process and get your team in the box as soon as you can. The Bcube"! experience is another innovative way to help teams develop their organizational learning capability. Each team that uses the Bcube"! process adapts it for its own use, creating new ways to use it. I look forward to seeing the development of even more innovative techniques for promoting out of the box thinking.

David P. Kruetzner
President of GKA

Acknowledgments

I know that whatever success is achieved will be due largely to the willingness of others to let me learn from them, and stand on their shoulders. The list below is only the beginning. I offer my sincere and deepest gratitude to the following people:

My wife, Willette, and family for their encouragement and patient support while I pursued my dreams, and especially to my son Ryan for his art work and creativity.

My brother, Herman Johnson, for his wisdom, guidance, and support.

Don McMillan, of APT Consulting, for his willingness to share great ideas.

Dr. Johnnie McFadden, a noted expert in transcultural diversity, but whom I will always remember as my seventh grade science teacher, for inspiring in me the search for excellence.

David Kreutzer, of GKA Incorporated for listening to my ideas, being willing to take a risk, and his ability to envision and talk about the future.

Captain Jerry Rodgers, the Charlotte Fire Department and Training Academy of Charlotte, NC, for the unselfish job that they perform, and for helping me appreciate the true meaning of the word "team".

Jackie Jones and Daniel Aronson for their editing ideas.

Dr. Nay Howell, for inspiring the ICS, Inc facilitators to

achieve, and for her positive outlook and influence.

Rachel Law, for her encouragement, her wisdom, her friendship, and for being willing to listen.

Joe Garnett, for being willing to take a risk.

My neighborhood prayer group, for their undying support.

Introduction

Organizations today are beginning to rely more and more on team-based processes to solve complex, multifaceted problems. But, how well do team members learn from each other? Are they able to share their insights with their peers? Are they able to form a shared vision or collective picture of the critical issues that confront them?

You may never know the answers to these critical questions until the group is thrown into the fire of a real-life situation. It is good to learn from experience, but by the time a team has an experience, it is usually too late to do anything about it, unless the problem occurs again. Imagine how much more effective the team could be if the skills needed to address an issue could be developed and practiced before having to use them in a real-life, and in real-time.

Since 1994, the Bcube™ process has been used as a tool to help organizations such as the Johns Hopkins Hospital Marburg Pavillion Nursing Staff, the Queens College Executive MBA Program, Charlotte City Government Employees, the Allstate Eastern Regional Data Center, and the Tamrock Corporation answer these kinds of questions, and gain valuable insights into the dynamics of teams and working groups of various sizes and make-up.

Participants experiencing the Bcube™ process see their deeply held assumptions, or mental models, held up to the light. They come face-to-face with their preconceived notions about their teammates, about themselves, and about what it means to work in a collaborative way with others. Groups start to understand the power and importance of developing a shared vision. This is precisely the kind of practice field experience that every team should have before encountering critical situations in real-life.

Bcube™ serves as an experiential point of entry to the learning process. It allows teams to test and examine their mental models about who they are, how they operate, and what they are able to accomplish together.

I believe that the observations contained here barely scratch the surface of the potential of using Bcube™ in settings where people interact with people. I believe there are valuable applications in such areas as family and couples counseling, touch therapy for the aged, providing a safe environment for exploring psychological and personality profiles, therapy for physically challenged individuals, and so on.

I hope that the ideas contained here will encourage others to explore the world of Bcube™ uses beyond my own mental models.

1

"Team" is a Four-Letter Word

For the average employee, "team" is a four-letter word —just another initiative driven by managers who are constantly trying to solve the problem of generating increased productivity at lower cost. It is put forward as the solution to problems that everyone in the organization knows exist, but whose solutions somehow always seem to be out of reach, if not totally out of focus. Sometimes employees feel as if they have managers who appear to be pulling remedies off the organizational development shelf and forcing them down employees' throats. Under such circumstances, it is not surprising that teamwork is perceived as nothing more than a passing initiative, like management by objectives, diversity, or Workforce 2000.[1]

Though organizational learning and other improvement initiatives have proven beneficial, they must clear a common organizational hurdle if their impact is to be fully realized: How do organizations get all of their employees mentally engaged and committed to making the process work? If an organization cannot get its employees committed, reaping the full benefits of any management process, no matter how good it is, will be difficult if not impossible.

These management tools are being used with varying degrees of success in many forms in corporations around the world. With the growing trend toward corporate downsizing and outsourcing, however, fewer and fewer employees are being asked to juggle more and more balls. Management groups are discovering that this juggling act becomes easier if they can develop a process in which learning is shared and collectively applied to the task at hand. When an organization learns to function in this way, the term that is used to describe its collective behavior and process is "team." As a result, many organizations are working to implement some version of team-based processes.

What Is Driving Organizational Processes?

It wasn't too long ago that organizations focused on doing business with people across the street, in their neighborhoods, across town, or perhaps in another part of the state. Then, with a broader range of customer needs, organizations were forced to begin thinking beyond their geographic boundaries. They found new competitors doing business in their own backyards. As a result, they recognized the need to think globally while acting locally. They began to find ways of competing in a geographically broader market while still providing personal, customized service.

Organizations are realizing that "change" is occurring more rapidly, and that they need to find ways of effectively responding to that change. It is estimated that the information learned by the average college graduate has a half life of four years. By the time that college student has worked for four years, half of everything that he or she learned while in college is obsolete. As a result, corporate America, which hires these graduates, must develop and institute processes that help their employees continue to learn. These organizations must themselves find ways to learn, and share that information across all functions.

Organizations are finding that their own customers, whether they are average consumers or a large corporate entity, are experiencing and being affected by change in their environments. How to measure that change as well as respond to it quickly and appropriately is a critical challenge faced by organizations of all types and sizes.

Another driver is the changing responsibility of employees, who are being asked to perform roles instead of jobs. There was a time when someone would ask me what I did for a living I would pull out my business card with my title displayed prominently beneath my name, and give it to him or her. The recipient would have a pretty good idea about the nature of my work. Now, when someone asks me what I do for a living, I find myself describing a series of roles that I play in order to meet the needs of my organization. Organizations are recruiting potential employees who are able to perform in multiple disciplines. Employees, who are able to wear many hats and still be effective, have become a most valued group within the corporate structure.

Finally, bosses are disappearing and coaches are beginning to emerge. Coaches don't play the game for the players. Coaches develop a structure within which the players can develop to their highest potential and contribute effectively to the success of the entire organization. The old structure, where the boss and the employee played what amounted to a professional game of fetch, is rapidly disappearing. This is where the boss identified the assignments, selected the people, and sent them out to perform a specific, structured task, and to then report back to him. Now organizations want people who can think, and who can add to the value of the organization by their ability to make good decisions quickly and wisely. These people need a clear vision of where the organization is trying to go, but they don't need to be told specifically what to do to get it there. They need coaches who are able to create an atmosphere and an organizational structure where they can perform and contribute to their fullest potential.

Why Is Structure Important?

The pace of business today is faster. In the past, the threat of competition came primarily from local competitors. With the passing of NAFTA and other trade agreements, competition is becoming more global. With the increasing numbers of females, minorities, nationals, and people from a broader range of academic disciplines moving into corporate positions, the face of the workplace, as well as of customers and competitors, is changing. These changes are rapidly making the traditional ways of managing people, doing business, and meeting the challenge of the market less and less effective. The old rules of the game are being challenged, and are quickly disappearing. New rules of the game are being written and rewritten every day. Change is the only dependable constant.

What most leaders are looking for is a way to make the greatest impact on their organization's profitability and productivity, at the lowest possible cost, and in the shortest possible time. Traditionally, efforts to accomplish this have been centered in one or more of these four areas:

- Vision: In what direction do we want to go, and where do we want to be?
- Strategic intent: What do we want to be?
- Strategy: How do we get there?
- Alignment: What infrastructure (people and processes) do we use to make it happen?

While all of these areas are important, leaders need to understand that each affects the organization differently, and that each area operates on its own relative impact timetable (see Figure 1).

What is the relative rate of organizational change?

Low

Rate of change

- Vision: In what direction do we want to go?
- Strategic Intent: What do we want to be?
- Strategy: How do we get there?
- Alignment: What structure do we use?

High

Figure 1

Vision statements exist in nearly every organization. Often they come about when a high-level group of managers meets for hours on end, sometimes days, to discuss, write, and word-smith where they think the organization should be heading. Usually, the group will pull out a classic vision statement, like President John F. Kennedy's vision of "sending a man to the moon, and returning him safely in this decade," and use it as an example, a role model of how a good vision statement should read and what elements it should contain. Once the vision statement is written and agreed on, it gets shared with the employees in a company ceremony, printed, matted, put in an expensive frame of exotic wood, and hung in the foyer of the corporate offices. Of course, every manager in the company who wants to show allegiance, support, and commitment to the vision has a smaller version hanging on his or her wall. This is all very important, but unfortunately, for many organizations, this is about as far as being visionary goes.

The problem that most organizations have is that few people in the organization can actually tell you what the vision is. Few employees can articulate it. If it can't be articulated, the chances are that it has not been internalized. It is not part of the culture of that organization. Visions are often so general that if you went into the lobby of ten similar corporations in the middle of the night and switched them, it would probably take a month before anyone noticed that they had been changed. Unfortunately, the most distinguishable differences in the vision statements of most companies are the frames in which they hang.

The vision is important, but if managers expect a change in the vision statement alone to motivate employees to keep pace with their competitors and their customers, they are in for a big disappointment. If a change occurs at all, it will be very slow. By the time it occurs, competitors and customers will have passed them by. If an organization is looking to bring about change, a clear, shared vision is essential, but vision alone cannot accomplish what is needed.

Strategic Intent and Strategy

The next critical step is to develop a strategic intent. What do we want to be? The difficulty most groups have with strategic intent is that they often confuse it with the strategy. Many organizations will invest a great deal of time, and money, and call in high-powered consultants to help them develop a strategy. Some organizations have entire departments devoted to what they call strategic planning. But most strategies, no matter how detailed and elaborate, rarely achieve their full potential because they are developed around a vision statement rather than a statement of strategic intent. The vision is intentionally broad and long-range— quite different from the strategic intent, which must be clear, concise, and focused.

What a strategy seeks to do is match the organization's resources with its opportunity. It is a balancing act where the available human resources and capital become the critical factors in determining just how aggressive the organization can afford to be in the marketplace. This is an exercise in resource accounting. A group of strategists decides how it will approach the available opportunities, given the perceived strength of the competitors, the projected growth of the market, its current and potential resources, and its limitations.

On the other hand, the strategic intent crystallizes the vision statement. It seeks to create a mismatch between opportunity and resources. It creates a healthy stretching of the organization's view of itself, and what it wants to become relative to its competitors and customers. It is not limited to the current human and capital resources, or current core competencies. Instead, it seeks to establish a creative tension, which motivates and invigorates the organization to reach beyond its grasp. It is around the strategic intent that the employees in an organization are mentally engaged.

Organizational Alignment

While the vision, strategic intent, and strategy are all critical to the success of an organization, it is the organizational alignment that largely determines the level of success the organization will achieve. It is the people who make an organization work. While vision, strategic intent, and strategy help set the direction of the work, the organizational alignment defines what the work is, how it will be done, and by whom.

Visions may change over the life of a company. The strategic intent may change over the life of a set of core competencies or market conditions. The strategy may change or be revised on a yearly basis, but the organizational alignment may be changed at any time. Small tweaks can be made in the system, or large moves can occur in the structure whenever internal or external conditions warrant. The organizational alignment is the area where changes occur most often, and where changes are expected to have the greatest impact.

The relative position of these four areas is very much like the beach balls in a basket at the toy store. The balls near the top of the basket can be removed or added without significantly disturbing the balls beneath them. If the balls near the bottom of the basket are disturbed, however, all the other balls will move in response.

The vision and the strategy of an organization may change with little immediate effect on the work of the average employee. It is impossible, however, for the employees and the way they interact with each other to change without having an effect on the direction and the level of success of the company. If an organization is ever to have maximum impact at minimal cost and in minimum time, it must tap into the potential found in the effective alignment of the people who work there.

There are many organizations that overlook this simple principle. Some believe that the way to have the greatest impact on the performance of the organization is to upgrade the technology. They spend millions of dollars each year traveling around the world, trying to find the latest and greatest technology. When they find it, they install it at the home facility. It often happens, however, that once the new technology is installed, the company does not reap 100 percent of the expected or projected benefit. When this occurs, an executive may ask the project leader whether the group might have missed some key part of making the technology work during their search, or if the seller has held back some key information, hoping to make more money selling a keyhole to a company that has already purchased a key. The company then starts a new project, this time with its best and brightest engineers. Their task is to figure out how to get the new multimillion-dollar technology to perform at the promised level.

What companies often fail to realize is that the success and impact of any process is not determined by technology alone. It is determined by how well technology is blended with the skills of its people, and how those people are then aligned within the organization to carry out their responsibilities (see Figure 2). To achieve maximum effectiveness, technology must be blended with the culture and alignment of an organization. This blend allows core competencies to emerge. The highest degree of control in any organization and the greatest point of influence is in the alignment of its people. A core competency results when technology and the skills of employees are blended and aligned in such a way that they produce a unique, sustainable, competitive advantage.

What are the areas of greatest organizational control?

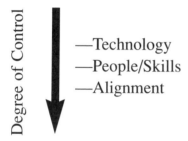

—Technology
—People/Skills
—Alignment

Figure 2

If we had enough money, we could duplicate the physical facilities and technology of GM, IBM, or 3M. That does not mean, however, that we would be able to manufacture products at the same level of quality, consistency, and innovation as these companies. What allows them to do what they do is the unique way in which they blend technology with the skills and alignment of the people who work for them. In fact, there are many companies with less in the way of technology that are very competitive with respect to quality, consistency, and innovation, because they have learned how to apply the power of blending employee skills and organizational alignment.

Organizational alignment simply means having the right people working together, in the right place, doing the right things, at the right time. When a company understands this and begins to act like its most important resource is its people, it starts to tap into a resource that has the power to convert vision statements into something that has value beyond the cost of the expensive frames in which they hang. A properly aligned workforce has the power to transform a vision into reality. People are generally the most underutilized and yet the most critical variable in a business's growth and performance.

2

The Development of a Team

One of the greatest hurdles that senior management groups face is knowing how to give employees the right information about the nature and conditions of the business in such a way that it motivates them to support corporate goals, decisions, and initiatives. This is especially tough when those decisions directly affect the average employee while often appearing to have little impact on the lives of the senior management group. If the senior management group is unable to get the employees engaged in the vision, then the likelihood that that vision will ever be realized is extremely small.

This difficulty gets further magnified in today's business culture, where the 1960s and 1970s versions of employee loyalty and job security are quickly disappearing. Organizations are beginning to adopt a strategy of strengthening their core competencies and outsourcing noncritical functions.

This is done as a popular method of reducing costs, while maintaining or increasing productivity. It was reported in *Business Week*[1] that in 1992, only 58 percent of Fortune 500 companies outsourced parts of their operation. In 1996, that number had jumped to 92 percent.

Today, the typical organizations that start up new facilities are weighing the virtues of buying versus leasing. Should they buy or lease a computer system? Should they buy or lease a phone system? Should they buy a building or lease space? And, last but not least, should they buy employees in the form of full-time workers or lease employees through an outsourcing strategy? The organization's bottom line is,"How do we continue to earn a profit and remain competitive in to-day's fast-paced, global economy? We will do whatever it takes to stay in business and provide products and services to our customers at a competitive price, while keeping our operating costs low."

Of course, it's difficult to get the average employee to buy in to such business moves, because from where he or she sits, moves like outsourcing mean the potential loss of employment. The employee's bottom line is, "If the organization no longer cares about me, then why should I care about the organization? Why should I work any harder than I have to in order to survive?"

It is in this climate of a fast-paced, competitive global economy that organizations are recognizing the need to find proven methods of doing more with less. As a result, reengineering efforts have become popular all over the world. Organizations are working to discover the benefits of operating in a team-based structure. They want to know how to reap those benefits.

Unfortunately, however, there seems to be a major disconnect between the impact that organizations project that reengineering and team efforts will have on costs and profitability, and what the real numbers show on the bottom line. James Champy, the noted co-author of the book *Reengi-*

neering the Corporation: A Manifesto for Business Revolution, estimates that only 30 percent of all reengineering efforts reap the full benefit of their potential.[2] The April 1, 1996 issue of *Business Week* magazine suggests that while outsourcing efforts on average promise 20 to 40 percent savings, the average savings are in reality only about 9 percent.[3]

In a later *Wall Street Journal* interview, the other co-author of *Reengineering the Corporation: A Manifesto for Business Revolution,* Michael Hammer, stated that while it was certainly correct to look at corporations and the work processes within those corporations from an engineering viewpoint, and to look at changing the flow of work so that it occurred more efficiently, a critical component was overlooked in their equation: people. In the article, Hammer states, "The real point of this is longer-term growth on the revenue side. It's not so much getting rid of people. It's getting more out of people. I . . . was insufficiently appreciative of the human dimension. I've learned that's critical."[4]

Organizations are trying to find ways to improve the output of their reengineering efforts. They are trying to find ways to reap a bigger percentage of the promised savings from outsourcing. They are recognizing the importance of getting every person in the organization mentally engaged. Brain power, especially in a downsized organization, is the one resource they cannot afford to leave untapped. These are the challenges.

To meet these challenges, many organizations are beginning to look more closely at the team process as a means of harnessing and refocusing the energy of employees. What makes a team work? What makes a team fail? What causes a team to be effective? But like so many initiatives that seem like great ideas in the boardroom, pushing the idea of a team-based culture can be much more difficult than it appears. Getting buy-in from employees to support organizational change is no easy task. After all, it is probably not immediately obvious to average employees that this move is going to be of any direct benefit to them.

So while the organization is trying to push forward with needed changes, its employees are pushing back on the organization. The result is an operating stalemate. This is very dangerous because in today's competitive business environment, a corporation does not have to move backward to lose ground in the marketplace—it only needs to stand still. When a company stands still, its competitors and their customers will quickly move ahead.

The Bcube™ process is designed to break this stalemate. It is designed to create an atmosphere where a greater sense of responsibility and ownership is developed and shared by employees and senior management.

What to Expect

While a team-based process may make perfect sense to the management group, implementing a team-based process may raise some serious questions in the minds of the average employee. If management fails to communicate why it believes that teams are important, and what will be the expected impact on employees and on the organization, it will be impossible to get employees engaged and committed to making the process work. There is a level of literacy about the business and decisions made about the business that management must effectively communicate to employees. All employees must have adequate business literacy if the organization is going to be successful in getting them mentally engaged in the process and personally committed to making it work. When an organization decides to move toward a team-based culture, several concerns will be raised in the minds of employees. Let's look at some of these.

Typical Concerns Members Have about Teams

"Teams" will often be seen as strictly a management initiative. As a result, employees may adopt a "this, too, shall pass" attitude. For many organizations, this occurs because employees know that the average life span of a senior management administration is two to three years. This being the case, average employees know that they will probably outlive the senior management administration that was responsible for the initiative. A typical employee strategy, then, is to do nothing and to wait out the tenure of the administrative group. A change at the top will eventually come, and a new initiative will soon replace the current one.

Once management shows that they are committed to establishing a team-based culture, some employees will perceive teams as "management passing the buck" of responsibility. Let's face it: employees in a team-based culture often find themselves taking actions and making decisions that at one time only managers could make. Why should employees want to take on bigger headaches, and greater responsibility, for the same pay? Besides, if the employees are successful, the effect will be less work for the boss or supervisor. Why should employees want to make the boss's job easier at the expense of their own jobs?

Sooner or later, employees will get to the bottom line, and ask, "What will adopting and supporting a team-based culture do for me as an employee? I understand what the impact will be on the organization and our customers, but what's in it for me personally? What do *I* get out of this deal?"

Most employees have been taught and rewarded for learning how to perform a job alone, with confidence and consistency. They have also been rewarded on the basis of how well this was done. As a result, employees will often be uncomfortable with this collaborative approach to work as a means of getting input and sharing learning with fellow employees. The general paradigm will be that collaboration is analogous to having someone look over an employee's shoulder or second guess an employee's best efforts. "If I have been doing my job, and performing acceptably, why do I need someone to help me now?"

In organizations where employees have become used to being rewarded for their individual contributions, they will want to know how they will be recognized for contributions in the new, team-based culture. They will want to know whether they can trust their ideas and suggestions to their team members. Will their ideas be seen as important? Will they get proper credit for their contributions? Will they be criticized for their ideas if their suggestions do not pan out or are unsuccessful? These are typical concerns employees may have about what it means to work in today's competitive organizations.

If an organization is to be successful in developing effective, high-performance teams and team-based processes and cultures, it must find a way of building a framework for a new set of mental models. As this framework for the new mental models begins to take shape, the team will experience a series of events that are indicators that will help the team know that it is on the right track.

It is very important that the senior management group show a strong, visible commitment. In the end, management will only get what they model, what they measure, and what they reward.

What Will Teams Experience?

After a team has been formed, and its members have been mentally engaged, it will experience a series of successes that come in baby steps. This is very good. A difficulty, however, may arise from the fact that a group of highly motivated individuals who have come together with clear goals and a shared vision generally wants to make giant leaps forward. They may become discouraged if their efforts are not producing headline-making results as quickly as they had hoped.

It is critical for the team to remember that before it can leap tall buildings in a single bound, it must first be able to step over the cracks in the road and up onto the curb. Baby steps are important, especially during the early stages of team development. Every giant leap has its origin in a baby step. If a team is ever going to make giant leaps, it is imperative that team members learn how to recognize, celebrate, and encourage successful baby steps. Baby steps may not get the team as far as it wants to go, but they are strong indicators that the team is moving in the right direction.

As the team begins to experience a series of successful baby steps, team members will begin to feel empowered to take on greater risks and responsibilities. Celebrated baby steps will bolster the team's confidence in its collective ability to make things happen in a new and meaningful way. The more success team members experience at any level, the more challenges they will seek out and be capable of meeting.

The team will gradually become more comfortable participating in decision-making processes, and may choose to get involved in such tasks as scheduling projects, assignments, and interviewing prospective team members.

As the team begins to feel comfortable pushing on the system, the system may start to feel uncomfortable and begin to push back on the team. Employees who are not part of the team may view with some envy the autonomy the team appears to have. They may believe that the team's apparent autonomy is a challenge to the system's policies, and that these challenges need to be addressed. Strong sponsorship is needed here. One of the key roles of the team's sponsor will be to act as a buffer to keep the organization adequately informed and to encourage the team.

The team will discover that the extent to which it grows, develops, and contributes to the productivity and growth of the organization will be largely determined by the boundaries the team imposes on itself. Team members will have mental models and paradigms about themselves and their own skills and capabilities. The team must constantly explore and challenge both real and perceived boundaries. It is often in examining these boundary areas that opportunities for improvement present themselves.

Interventions such as Bcube™ allow teams to simulate group interaction in a safe, nonthreatening environment. It allows them to test and examine their mental models about who they are, how they operate, and what they are able to accomplish together. It allows them to continually challenge and reshape these mental models in a way that helps the team learn and be productive.

3

The Bcube™ Experience

What is Bcube™?

Bcube™ is a patented learning device designed to allow people to experience the process of discovering their mental models, and learning how to convert this experience into increased productivity and a competitive advantage (see Figure 3). While the primary focus in this discussion is on business work groups, the tool can be equally as effective when applied to any group that wants to mentally engage its members around the importance of working together to reach a common goal.

Figure 3
Bcube™ Photograph

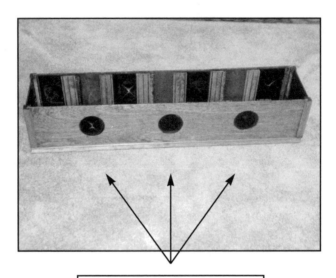

3 of 7 Touch Points
Access to Workstations

Bcube™ is a rectangular box measuring approximately fourty-eight inches long and fifteen inches high. It is constructed so that the inside is divided into as many as seven compartments or workstations, separated by a "U"-shaped spacer. Access to each workstation is gained through a hole in the side of Bcube™ known as a touch point (see Figures 4–6). The touch point is large enough for the average adult hand to be easily inserted and move about freely. The workstations and corresponding touch points are arranged so that the person whose workstation is next to a participant is actually the person who is sitting across from that participant. This promotes eye contact among the members of the teams as they perform the various exercises.

Figure 4
Bcube™ Side View

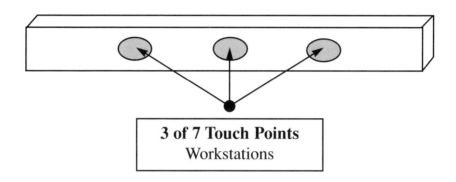

3 of 7 Touch Points
Workstations

Figure 5
Bcube™ Top View

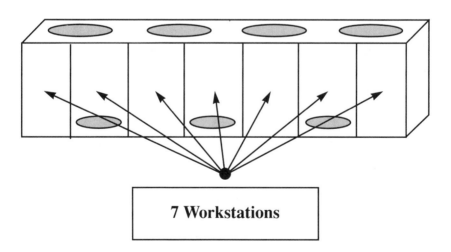

7 Workstations

Figure 6
Bcube™ Top View

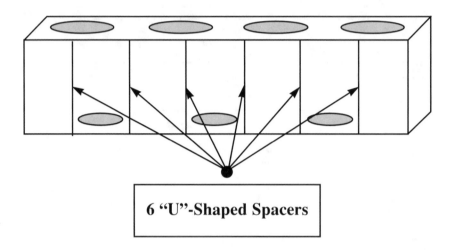

The Boundary of Touch

In experiencing the Bcube™ process, participants insert their hands into the box through the touch points and then carry out a variety of exercises that are designed to break down communication barriers and increase the level of mutual trust. Bcube™ is designed so that the first barrier the participants have to overcome is the barrier of touch. Although there is enough space around the outside of Bcube™ for seven adults to work comfortably, the nature of the activities and the construction of the inside of Bcube™ make it necessary for the hands of the participants to touch as they engage in the various exercises.

For many, especially for those in Western cultures where touching is thought to be an intrusion into one's personal space, the constant touching inside the box as the exercises unfold may at first be somewhat uncomfortable, but is a significant point of learning. This may be especially true when teams are composed of all male participants, male and female participants, or participants from different ethnic groups. Touching is the first step in bringing down social, cultural, and personal barriers. It helps bring down facades and ease the tension among the participants. After the first exercise, people begin to relax and be themselves.

In performing the exercises, participants learn that touching inside the box, along with the eye contact around Bcube™, provides teams with an important means of subtly giving and receiving encouragement. They discover that it is also a very effective means of giving and receiving positive and constructive feedback.

These logistics in and of themselves do not move the group's learning forward. What they do is help create an environment where, when combined with the Bcube™ exercises, personal and collective discovery occurs on a significant emotional level that is as safe and nonthreatening as possible.

The Blind Men and the Elephant

There is an old Indian fable in which several blind men encounter an elephant. Depending on what part of the elephant they touch, they each form a different mental picture, or "mental model," of what the elephant looks like. (The term "mental model" is used to describe each person's view of reality. It describes how we perceive the world around us.)

The one who grabs the trunk, because it is long and squirmy, thinks an elephant must be like a snake. The one who grabs the tusk, because it is long, smooth, and sharp, thinks that an elephant must be like a spear. The one who grabs the ear, because it is wide, flat, and waves back and forth, thinks that an elephant must be like a fan, and so on.

All these blind men are exactly right, in a sense. Parts of an elephant are like these objects, but at the same time, they are all completely wrong.

In a sense, the blind men are operating like a dysfunctional organization or team. They represent a team in which everyone is working hard, doing their individual part, but they have not figured out how to pull their efforts together so that they are able to accomplish more collectively than they are able to accomplish as individuals.

If they could find a way to share their individual images or mental models of the elephant with each other, and could somehow develop a new, collective team mental model, they could probably come up with a fairly good representation of what an elephant really looks like. Now, of course, their collective mental model would not look exactly like an elephant, but it would certainly look more like an elephant than their individual mental images.

What Bcube™ does is take the type of experience represented by the blind men and the elephant and convert it into a series of tabletop exercises. In these exercises, groups or teams are able to share a similar mental model experience and the opportunity for learning that those blind men experienced. They are led to understand how important it is to work together, developing collective mental models and a shared vision around these collective mental models. With Bcube™, groups don't just talk about the theory and concept of teams; they experience what it *feels* like to successfully operate as a real team and, ultimately, as a high-performance team.

Why Does Bcube™ Work?

As illustrated by the behavioral ray model in Figure 7, developed by Don McMillan and Dave Gordon of APT Consulting,[1] most behaviors grow out of experience. By experience I mean some significant emotional event occurs in the life of an individual, a team, or an organization. When an experience is internalized, a belief is formed that begins to establish that experience and its outcomes as a rational fact.

Once a belief is established, a strategy is then formed to help explain why things are the way they are. Internal criteria are established as a forecasting mechanism to check and predict when conditions in a new experience are most likely to

Where do most behaviors originate?

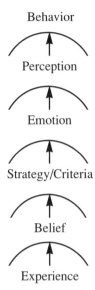

Behavior

Perception

Emotion

Strategy/Criteria

Belief

Experience

For the most part, behavior is experience-based

Figure 7

lead to an anticipated or similar outcome. These criteria can be used to test influences entering the environment to see whether they fit with previously observed patterns of events.

When the strategy/criteria mechanism is established and validated by observing the outcomes of a series of experiences, the belief system becomes part of the emotions and begins to form the value system. That value system then begins to define how we see, interpret, and filter all of the incoming data from the world around us. This is where mental models are most important. As we experience the workings of the world around us, our mental models represent the standard to which we hold those experiences. They are the polarizers through which we filter our ideas of work, friendship, security, marriage, and so on. Once the incoming data have been decoded, interpreted, and cataloged under a mental model from experience, a suitable response or behavior is identified, brought to the surface, and implemented. Personal styles develop in very much the same way. This process occurs every day, in every personal and professional setting and interaction.

For example, imagine that Fred is a new employee at the Acme Chemical Co. After he has been working there for a few days, the CEO schedules a general meeting where he announces that Acme will begin practicing openness and trust at all levels in the organization. He invites each employee to say just what's on his or her mind. Jennifer raises her hand and asks, "Why can't we have greater access to information about the financial performance of the company? How much money do we make? How do we reinvest our profits? The information we're getting is sketchy, and lacks the kind of substance employees need to draw accurate conclusions about the financial health of Acme."

This hits a nerve with the CEO. He shoots back, "*I* am the CEO of this company. Understanding the financial details of this operation is my responsibility, not yours. If you feel you are not getting the information you need to perform your job satisfactorily, then you might consider looking for another job. Next question, please."

Well, with a response like that, you can imagine that the number of questions is quickly reduced. This experience tells Fred that although the written policy from the CEO talks about trust and openness, this is far from the actual culture within the organization. As a result, Fred's practiced behavior becomes closed and nonsharing. Fred's experience leads him to a behavior of self-preservation and inward focus.

Fred's approach to the organization becomes very much like that of the cat that jumps up after sitting on a hot stove. Through that experience, the cat learns not to sit on a hot stove. Unfortunately, since for the most part, all stoves look alike to a cat, the cat learns not to sit on any stove, hot or cold, because the consequences of testing the conditions of the stove are greater than the cat is willing to risk. The cat's experience has helped shape and determine the cat's behavior. If, like the cat, Fred sees the risk of asking good questions as being greater than the potential payback, he—and ultimately the organization—will be cheated of critical learning.

Now, let's suppose you drive home from work pretty much along the same route every day. You have taken this route so often that you could almost follow it with your eyes closed. One day, however, you're on your way home, and you look in your rearview mirror. A set of flashing red and blue lights has pulled up behind your car. You get a sick feeling in the pit of your stomach. A police officer pulls you over and gives you a ticket for doing 55 in a 45 mph zone. While you're sitting in the police officer's car waiting for him to finish the paperwork, several of your friends from work pass by and see you. You begin to sweat.

If something like this has ever happened to you, it's a pretty safe bet that in the future, every time you come to that section of road, you're going to slow down, even if you are not exceeding the speed limit. Your new behavior is being generated by your experience with the police officer.

The Experience/Behavior Relationship

When the experience/behavior process is diagrammed, the underlying relationships become more evident.

Figure 8
Event/Experience Diagram

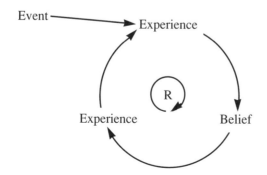

In Figure 8, we see that the experience is actually triggered by an event. Something happens that changes or intro-
duces a new set of conditions to the environment in which
the person or the organization is functioning. In the previous
example, looking in the rearview mirror and seeing a set of
flashing red and blue lights behind you is the event. In this
case the event is so significant that it generates that heart-
pounding, nauseating feeling in the pit of your stomach.

This heart-pounding, nauseating feeling marks the beginning of your unpleasant experience. The experience includes things like nervously trying to find your driver's li-
cense and registration, wondering why the officer has
stopped you, watching your co-workers look at you as they
pass by, and so on.

Figure 9
Experience/Behavior Diagram

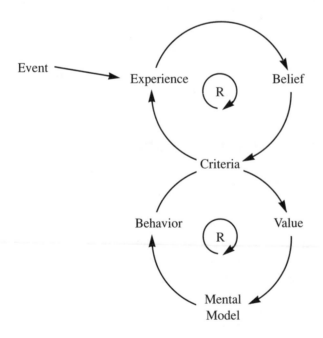

The experience, then, begins to shape your belief about several things. It will begin to shape your belief about that particular stretch of road. Your belief about police officers will be shaped by whether you thought this officer was friendly, for example.

As the diagram indicates, the belief system formed from one event may not be strong enough to move all the way through the system. In such instances, it may be necessary for other events to occur to reinforce and eventually solidify the belief. In other instances, the event may be so significant that the belief system reaches critical mass and gels almost immediately.

If the time between events is sufficiently long, the reinforcing loop may develop so slowly that it may be difficult to form a clear belief. In these cases, the event may lead to the formation of a superstition rather than a rational belief based on hard data.

Let's assume that the event generates a significant experience and galvanizes the belief system. The next step is the establishment of an internal strategy or a set of criteria that fits the belief, and the description of the conditions under which an event will repeatedly generate the observed experience. These then lead to the formation of values that shape our mental models or perceptions (see Figure 9). As stated earlier, mental models determine how we see the world and how we interpret the events that occur in the world around us. There may be several mental model catalogs or files related to a certain event. These catalogs are dependent on the conditions under which that event and resulting feelings occurred. Once the internal filing system has decided under which category an event is to be filed, the resulting behavior is almost a natural output.

Systemically, however, there is an important closure to the causal loop diagram that is often overlooked. That closure is the link between the behavior of a person, organization, or department and the experience of another. In effect, the behavioral output of one person or group becomes the event that triggers the experience of another person or group (see Figure 10). This is why it is often observed that the problem solved in department 'A' without regard to the total system creates new problems for departments 'B' and 'C.' There is no isolated behavior. Every behavior becomes the catalyst for some other experience base. Sometimes this is intentional. Sometimes it is unintentional, but it happens nevertheless.

In the speeding motorist example, it is the motorist's behavior that provides the event that triggers the experience for the police officer. The officer probably filtered his observations through his belief system and criteria to form some judgment as to whether this was a drunk driver, a fleeing criminal, or a person who was just a little too anxious to get home from work. The officer put the motorist into a mental

Figure 10
Behavior/Event Diagram

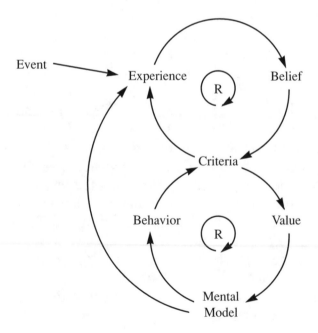

model category. This mental model determined with how much caution the car should be approached, whether his revolver should be drawn, whether backup was needed, and so on. The officer's final behavior was to stop the car. At that point, then, the officer's behavior was the event that triggered the motorist's experience. And so the system continues to emerge.

This event-experience-behavior-event process has universal application. When the process is applied to the observation of natural phenomena, it is called physical science. It is through these kinds of relationships that scientists form hypotheses and theories. If these theories are observed with some constancy, they become scientific laws. They all have their roots in the event-experience-behavior relationship. When this process is applied to people, it is called behavioral psychology. When the process is applied to a commu-

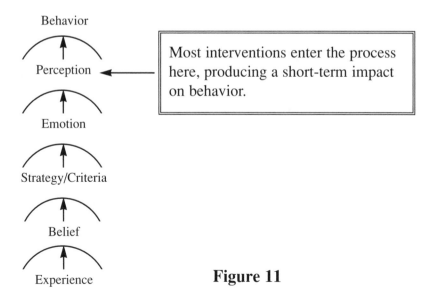

A Typical Approach to Impacting Behavior

Behavior

Perception ← Most interventions enter the process here, producing a short-term impact on behavior.

Emotion

Strategy/Criteria

Belief

Experience

Figure 11

nity, it is called organizational learning and results in the formation of cultural norms.

In many organizations, when it is decided that a different behavior is needed around some set of critical issues, they begin searching for an intervention that will help change the group's perceptions (see Figure 11). Entering at the perception level, they try to change the way the group sees themselves. They want to change the way they view their fellow employees. They want to change the way they see their jobs. They want to change the way they see their customers. The organization hopes that by working on employees' perceptions, they will be able to generate enough logic, motivation, and buy-in to push for a different response or behavior.

When an attempt is made to change a group's perception, an effort to practice the desired behavior may be observed for a while. After two or three months, however, the new behavior has faded and the old behavior has returned. This occurs because even though the new initiative has had an impact on the organization's perception, the organization may still be operating from the old experience base. If the old experience base is the only operating base the organization knows, that experience base will continue to drive the individual or the group toward the old behavior.

If a new experience base is not established, the old experience base will keep pushing forward. Eventually, the belief system, the strategy, and the emotions emanating from the old experience base overtake the new perceptions, and the old behavior slowly begins to surface again.

The Need for a Common Experience Base

One of the most effective methods for generating a different behavior is to create a new experience (see Figure 12). If you can get people to share a common experience base, then their new behavior will be a natural outcome of that experience. The new experience will generate its own set of beliefs, strategies, emotions, perceptions, and, finally, behavior.

Notice that the new experience does not try to change or overcome the old behavior. This is very difficult, if not impossible, because the event that led to the experience can't be changed. It happened, and we're stuck with it. An event or an experience cannot be undone. Instead, the new experience generates its own set of beliefs, strategies, and perceptions, and, finally, an alternative to the old behavior emerges. The new experience creates a behavioral choice, identifying an alternative road. The group does not have to fix the old road. They only have to choose to take the new road. What the Bcube™ process does is enter at the experience level.

Most high-performance teams have had a shared or common experience base. They generally have had some core

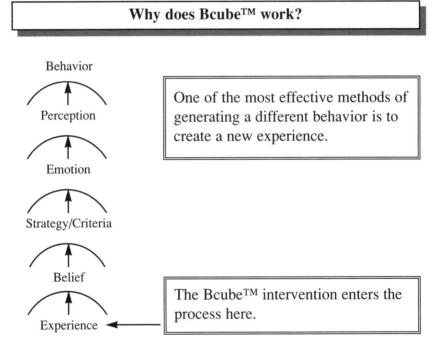

Figure 12

experience from which they can move forward to a high level of concerted behavior.

In the case of the Marines, their shared experience base is boot camp. In boot camp, the drill instructors don't waste time trying to change old values and perceptions. Instead, they work to instill new values by providing a common experience base.

Most of the time when we think of boot camp, we believe that its purpose is to train recruits to be soldiers. It is certainly true that training is a critical element, but in addition to training, these soldiers come together to develop a core experience, from which all other performance emanates. They wear the same clothes, they eat the same food, they get up at the same time, they go to bed at the same time, and they have the same haircuts. Virtually everything that they do is designed to replace individualism with an esprit de corps that creates a common experience base. The soldiers are bonded through that common experience base.

They exist collectively as a high-performance team, not as individual experts. When the team has reached this point of development, their drill instructor and subsequent trainers are then able to develop them into soldiers who will respond in the desired way under any given set of circumstances.

When basic training is completed, the core experience of these soldiers has created a mental model that says that, if necessary, I can trust my life to those who share in this experience. When I am in danger, I can readily charge forward, because I totally trust the people who have been trained to watch my back to do exactly what they are supposed to do.

The application and impact of the common experience base are even observed biblically in the process that Jesus used to train his disciples. According to the Bible, this training occurred over a three-and-a-half year period. During this period they traveled together, ate together, talked together, and practiced a disciplined lifestyle together. Jesus did not seek to change their old behavior, but through the experience base he provided for them, he sought to develop a vision of a new standard of morality and behavior. The impact of this common experience base was a bond and a level of mutual trust that could not be broken, even by death.

There are times when businesses will experience something that creates a common experience base. This helps rally them to generate a new organizational behavior. Unfortunately, this usually occurs when the organization experiences some form of external competitive threat. The threat forces the organization to realize that a different behavior is critical to the company's survival.

The common experience base is one of the most powerful tools for uniting a group around a shared vision. We see it in nearly every high-performance team. It is effective and compelling. These examples clearly demonstrate how valuable this principle of the common experience base is to the success of high-performance teams. We have seen it in the arts, in the military, in sports, and in religion.

The challenge for businesses that want to stay on the competitive forefront is to learn how to apply this concept to business processes before there is a crisis sitting on the doorstep. Seek to develop and utilize the principle of the common experience base as a normal part of employee development, and as the first, critical step toward building a workforce that can produce extraordinary results under all business conditions.

4

Bcube™ and the Role of Mental Models

How Do Bcube™ Exercises Work?

Individuals and organizations experience the world through one or more of the five senses. The more sensory avenues that are engaged, the more powerful will be the impact of the experience on the belief system, the value system, perceptions, and, ultimately, behavior.

The Bcube™ process generates a set of experiential conditions that maximize the sensory avenues to learning. In addition, Bcube™ forms a sensory network among the participants, so that their common experience becomes a shared experience on a deeper, more personal level.

Some Typical Exercises

The unique design of Bcube™ provides participants with the experience of working in a team-based, learning culture, where experience enters through the senses of touch, sight, and hearing. Because the exercises are designed to engage multiple sensory avenues of the team and the team members, the common experience base tends to be stronger and of greater impact than that obtained through lecture, personality testing, role play, and other singular sensory interventions or processes.

The Bcube™ experience consists of several basic exercises: "Naming the Game," the "Mental Model Relay," "Exploring Mental Models," and "Building New Mental Models." These exercises are varied in order to address the special needs of a team or group of individuals.

NAMING THE GAME

In the "Naming the Game" exercise, the teams are asked to develop a team structure and strategy for moving an oblong ball one hundred yards. The barrier they have to overcome is another team of eleven men, who average 250 pounds and are trying to keep them from moving the ball.

This exercise is essentially designed to get people talking. It is used to break the ice and develop an initial level of communication among the members of the team. As teams work to develop a list of options for accomplishing the task, and then ultimately present their strategies to the other teams, facilitators get a glimpse into the dynamics of each group: Who assumes leadership? How well is the team listening to its members? Are every person's ideas heard and considered?

MENTAL MODEL RELAY

In the "Mental Model Relay," several objects are placed inside Bcube™. Without talking, the members of the team examine each object and write down what they think it is. If the members are not certain what the object is, they may draw a picture or use descriptive terms to create an image of what they believe the object to be. After each person has developed a list, the group is allowed to share their perceptions with their team members. The team then uses the collective data from its members to generate a consensus list.

This exercise is used to demonstrate the importance of getting total team involvement in making decisions. If a team member does not speak up very much, that does not mean that the team member has nothing to say. It is important to create an atmosphere that is safe enough to allow each team member to contribute openly and honestly. The process shows how critical it is in today's competitive climate to get every team member mentally engaged.

Team members' perceptions about who has useful information to share and who does not grow out of the mental models they have about each other. The dynamics observed in this exercise occur every day as participants at all levels in organizations sit in meetings around conference room tables, examining and debating a variety of issues. Many disagreements in this kind of setting grow out of the participants' different mental models or different perceptions about the issue at hand. The need in the conference room is the same as in this exercise: create an atmosphere where people feel safe enough to openly and honestly share their mental models with the rest of the team, without having to fear that their ideas may not be valued. The participants learn that no organization can afford to ignore another member's ability to contribute to achieving its business goals and objectives.

MENTAL MODEL CONSTRUCTION

In the "Mental Model Construction" exercise, a simple object is disassembled and placed inside Bcube™. Without removing the object from Bcube™, participants are asked to collaborate in putting the object back together.

This exercise is used to demonstrate the principles of strategic planning, leadership, and interactive, cross-functional communication among team members. These skills are critical to the successful completion of the project.

BUILDING NEW MENTAL MODELS

In the "Building New Mental Models" exercise, a structure is built and placed inside Bcube™. Working together, participants are asked to feel the structure inside the box and, using similar materials, build a copy of the structure outside the box. Bcube™ is constructed in such a way that team members have blind spots and must solicit assistance from other team members in order to complete their piece of the structure. Then, each participant must determine how his or her part of the structure connects with those of teammates.

This exercise gives participants experience in using the critical elements of open communication and trust while operating as a high-performance team. In this experience, team members gain valuable insights about themselves, about their teammates, and about how they work together.

Through self-assessment and facilitation processes, participants learn how their behaviors during the exercises mirror their behaviors in real life. However, because these behaviors are displayed in an atmosphere of play, often using children's toys, participants are able to recognize and talk about them in a way that is not threatening to the individual or the team. Once these behaviors are out in the open, the team can then learn how to apply their insights to day-to-day work situations.

Teams who go through the Bcube™ process experience several outcomes:

- A safe, nonthreatening atmosphere where personal and collective discovery can occur is created.
- More open communication among team members occurs.
- Teams are mentally engaged around a common experience base.
- Mutual trust is gained.

- A framework is built in which teams can begin to identify and explore critical issues and areas of conflict.
- Teams learn how to convert individual differences and mental models into a competitive advantage.

Why the Bcube™ Process Works

As I stated earlier, "mental model" is a term used to describe each person's view of reality. It describes how we interpret the world around us. Mental models develop and grow out of our backgrounds, the places we have been, the kind of books we read, the television programs we watch, and so on. In short, they are an outgrowth of the sum of our personal experiences.

Mental models influence how we make decisions. They influence how we approach our professional and personal lives, and provide the framework for what each of us calls "normal." We are all eyewitnesses to many events and situations in life. We discover, however, that like the eyewitnesses to an automobile accident or any public event, what is seen and experienced is unique to each person. As a result, there are as many mental models of reality as there are observers of reality. Conflicts in most personal and group interactions occur when these mental models clash. We are unwilling or unable to openly share what mental models shape our point of view. Learning how to have these kinds of discussions is the first step in a team's developing a new, collective mental model that each team member can support.

In business, a strategy is an organized response to a mental model about a perceived market opportunity. The success or failure of a strategy is often based on the strategists' ability to construct a mental model that is representative of the market and the competition.

Our personal relationships, friendships, and marriages are shaped by each person's mental model of love, family, and commitment. It wasn't too long ago that the term "family" meant Mom, Dad, 2.5 children, and a pet. Now, the concept of family includes single mothers, single fathers, childless couples, and more.

Bcube™ is an intervention that allows people to explore and understand how mental models shape and influence decisions in their professional and personal interactions. Bcube™ also allows people to experience the importance of working with others to develop collective mental models. Collective mental models are generally more accurate and lead to better decisions than those that result from group members working individually.

Mental models have their origin in our experiences, but their effect can only be observed in our behaviors. To effectively demonstrate the power and role of mental models in systems thinking, then, we must start at the experience level and then move forward to the perception level and finally to the behavior level. Bcube™ provides an experiential point of entry for learning about the role and power of mental models.

It has been noted that when children play, they are always playing on a make-believe adult level. Children never pretend to be children. They play to feel like adults, because they already know what it feels like to be children. When they play, they are making a mental transition from the real world of childhood to the imaginary world of adulthood.

It is during the act of play that children begin to form mental models about what it feels like to be a fire fighter, police officer, nurse, doctor, Mommy, Daddy, and so on. They observe the behavior of these people, and use those observations to form the framework of their mental models. New experiences or observations allow children to gather more data to build on this mental model foundation as they grow and learn.

As adults, we act on and react to current realities by comparing them with our mental models, making decisions based on how they compare. Our behaviors, then, are largely the result of these mental model comparisons.

Bcube™ uses various kinds of children's toys in many of the exercises. The result is that the adults who share in the Bcube™ experience are brought to a level of play that is not common in their day-to-day activities. As they approach this level of play, they bring with them their adult mental models of how they should behave and interact with friends, family members, peers, subordinates, and supervisors. They bring their mental models about teams, relationships, acceptance, and leadership. As they engage in these activities, their responses and behaviors begin to reflect these mental models.

Playing with toys is generally seen by adults as a safe, nonthreatening experience. As a result, during the exercises they begin to lower natural barriers and defenses, and their true selves and natural behaviors begin to emerge. These are the same behaviors they exhibit in day-to-day interactions, roles, and responsibilities. Because of real or perceived personal risks, however, it may be difficult for adults to admit to these behaviors or for their colleagues to point them out. In the Bcube™ exercises, these behaviors begin to emerge and come to the surface, where they are observed and experienced by them and by their team members (playmates).

Instead of creating or projecting mental models like they did when they were children, adults bring their mental models and their resulting behaviors with them to the Bcube™ play experience. Because the group is in an attitude of play and in a relatively safe environment, it is easier for their mental model–driven behaviors to be realized, shared, and discussed freely and openly. The consequences of talking about their behavior during playtime are much less severe and less threatening than the consequences of raising such issues while performing real-life functions and responsibilities.

What Does Bcube™ Do?

What the Bcube™ experience does, then, is bring people face to face with their behaviors. It gradually constructs and polishes a mirror that allows participants to observe a reflection of their true, unfiltered selves in a safe, non-threatening environment. The Bcube™ experience raises the participant's behavioral responses to a conscious level, making it easier to identify and develop personal improvement strategies. The result is that participants perform more effectively in their real-world environments.

The Bcube™ experience can be used to form the foundation for leading a group into a variety of other critical discussion areas. Once participants have a greater awareness of what is driving and shaping their own perceptions and those of their colleagues, they are ready to talk on a more meaningful level about such issues as strategy, team building, diversity, and so on.

Using Bcube™ allows for a closer examination of the concept of mental models, and helps get buy-in to FAST-Break™ on an emotional level. When people experience Bcube™, they are opening up or at least broadening their avenues of creativity, innovation, self-confidence, and mutual trust. They are lowering the natural barriers to trust that come from the caution that develops as we grow older.

Employees in the workplace learn to be cautious. They learn how to minimize their risks, because they constantly live in an environment where one mistake could cost them their jobs or jeopardize their career and future. They develop a behavior of sharing only a small piece of their safe selves while holding in check the part that may indeed be most critical to solving a crucial problem or establishing a key relationship. This behavior occurs wherever there are group interactions. Employees thus cheat themselves, cheat their team members of themselves, and may perhaps be cheating the organization of a much-needed perspective.

If we take time to lower the natural barriers to trust and openness that exist between team members, we can be more effective in identifying the mental models on which such interventions as the FASTBreak™ process, and ultimately causal loops, are built.

Perhaps of greater importance, however, is the question of whether an organization or team will feel truly empowered to make the necessary changes in its business processes if it does not believe that the interventions like the FAST-Break™ process have accurately captured and reflected gut-level, critical issues. If this is not accomplished, the benefits of the process of change may not be fully realized. In this regard, Bcube™ serves as an experiential point of entry to the whole process of learning.

5

Anticipatory Learning

(Learning From the Future)

Expecting and Planning for the Unexpected

Once the team has completed the Bcube™ process, team members are ready to learn how to convert their new knowledge into a competitive advantage. Their objective is to develop the competencies of a high-performance team in a learning organization as described in Table 1.

Table 1
Competencies of a High-Performance Team
in a Learning Organization

1. Practice anticipatory learning
2. Achieve total organizational engagement

3. Create opportunities to share learning and practice skills
4. Exercise external vision while keeping an internal awareness
5. Trace every operation to a customer or market need
6. Understand core competencies
7. Cherish no sacred cows
8. Develop a business literate workforce: leaders are able to effectively transfer critical information to the workforce
9. Practice collaborative learning, with the ability to transfer learning within the organization
10. Establish continuous improvement processes
    Continually seek to know:
      • What's the name of the game?
      • Who's making the rules?
      • Who owns the ball?

Organizations often find themselves reacting to moves made in the marketplace by their competitors. They find themselves reacting to changes in the habits or expressed needs of their customers. If an organization can react quickly enough, it may be able to stay in business, but it tends to be in a perpetual, high-stress mode of catch-up. When this happens, the performance of employees at all levels of the organization begins to suffer.

It often happens that by the time an organization catches up, its competitors and customers may have moved on to someplace else. It is constantly trying to hit a moving target. If that scenario plays out too often, the organization will find itself out of business. It learns how to be reactive but never proactive.

It is generally accepted that organizations need to be able to learn and develop strategies in real time. They need to be creative and flexible enough to think on their feet, and be able to react as market and customer needs continue to evolve. Many organizations have been successful with this approach, but as the pace of business begins to move from local to global speed, they are finding it increasingly difficult to function in the reactive mode as their primary method of operation. More and more businesses are recognizing the need to be strategically proactive. They want to find a way of identifying and getting to the future before their competitors and customers do.

Real-time learning may be adequate to keep up with the game, but companies that are looking to the future want to know how to get ahead of the game. This means developing a different set of high-performance team skills called anticipatory learning, or learning from the future.

When organizations practice learning from the future, they are developing products and services that are consistent with their customers' future needs and strategically appropriate to their competitors' growing capabilities. They are realizing that today's products will probably not be adequate to meet tomorrow's market opportunities.

If the needs of the customers of an organization get to the future before the organization's capabilities to deliver those needs, customers will go where those new needs can be met. If an organization is going to remain competitive and successful over the long term, it must recognize that whoever gets to the customer's future first has the best chance of getting the customer's business.

What Is the FASTBreak™ Process?

FASTBreak™ is a systems thinking intervention that provides groups and individuals with a process for developing robust strategies that address critical, organizational, and personal issues.

I was introduced to the FASTBreak™ process in 1995 by David Kreutzer, president of GKA Incorporated.[1] Since then, I have successfully used it many times to think through and develop strategies for a variety of personal and business-related issues.

The first step in learning from the future is to brainstorm the critical issues affecting the customer, the company, the market, and the competition. This exercise is more effective after the planning group has gone through the Bcube™ exercises to get them grounded around a core experience base. Bcube™ also helps raise the level of trust and encourages open communication.

In the second step, the people, competitors, customers, and so on, who have a stake in how these issues are resolved, are identified. In this process, the planning group looks outside itself and steps into the mental models shoes of the stakeholders. In so doing, they try to assess how the stakeholders see these issues, and what actions they are predisposed to take in order to achieve their goals. What do they want, and what are they likely to do in order to get what they want?

In the third step, the planning group develops a range of options or actions based on the matrix they have developed for each stakeholder. This allows the planning group to assess the range of market opportunities and determine where their market opportunities are most likely to be found.

In the final step, the planning team develops a strategy that is robust and resilient to internal changes, changes in the market, and the actions taken by their competitors. Notice that the team is not trying to pinpoint a strategic thrust. Instead, they are trying to draw a bull's-eye around a set of related opportunities and options. The company aims for a point within the bull's-eye. The result is a set of strategic options that are robust and resilient enough to be able to incorporate midcourse corrections as external and internal conditions change.

There is no foolproof strategy. Somewhere during the execution of a strategy, external or internal conditions are likely to develop that make it necessary to make at least one midcourse correction. Aiming at the bull's-eye instead of focusing on a single point means that organizations are able to move toward their customers' future while maintaining the flexibility to make modifications as needed.

Practice, Practice, Practice

If a team is going to be able to apply its new skills effectively and consistently, it is critical that team members find a way to keep those skills sharp by practicing them on a regular basis. In fact, practice is an essential element of all high-performance team processes. This is true for teams in the performing arts, sports, the military, medicine, and so on. Wherever high-performing teams are found, a proven process of practice is almost certain to exist.

Practice provides an opportunity for teams to revisit their common experience base. Revisiting the common experience base helps reinforce the team's beliefs, validate its strategy and criteria, solidify its values, reframe its mental models, and make the desired behaviors part of the culture.

Practice gives teams the opportunity to learn while minimizing the consequences of mistakes. If the consequences of mistakes are too high, the creativity of the team may be stifled. Team members will be led to continually take the safe paths and may never discover just how far their capabilities can be stretched. They may never realize the opportunities they have to improve their processes.

When the consequences for making mistakes are low and the opportunity for learning is high, the team tends to be more willing to exercise creative freedom in problem-solving exercises. The team also tends to be more willing to continually test and redefine the limits of their skills and capabilities both as a collective group and as individuals.

For example, pilots for the major airlines are required to spend some time in the flight simulator on a regular basis. It has been observed that requiring a pilot to go back into the flight simulator after logging about 20,000 hours of flying time helps keep judgment and flying skills at peak performance. The flight simulator is designed to teach the pilot to fly. In addition, however, it is also designed to keep a pilot's flying and safety skills sharp, functioning at their absolute best. It allows pilots to resharpen their skills by revisiting their core experience base, and, as a result, gives them a better chance of maintaining peak flying performance.

In the flight simulator the pilot is able to test and reestablish the limitations of his or her competencies while keeping the risk of failure to a minimum. This learning is critical to the pilot's survival, but it is usually too dangerous and too late to explore for the first time during an actual flight emergency, especially if there are passengers on board the plane.

Like pilots, it is critical that all high-performance teams establish their version of a flight simulator. This is essential if they are going to keep their team skills at peak performance.

While the design of an actual simulator may be specific to the desired business outcomes of the team, Bcube™ exercises can be used as a relatively quick, simple process for allowing the team to reestablish a common experience base. From this base, teams can explore critical performance issues and examine and set new norms for both team and individual behaviors.

The other function of the flight simulator is to provide engineers with information on how an airplane should be constructed. This is done by studying the skills, capabilities, and limitations of pilots. Engineers can design an airplane that structurally can withstand greater G forces than the average pilot is able to take. Engineers also recognize that all pilots are not created equal. Some are clearly more capable than others. It is a simple fact of human nature that some pilots are aces and some are not.

Therefore, if you are an engineer designing a functional airplane, you don't want to design an airplane that only aces can fly. You want to design one that your worst pilot on his or her worst day can climb into, take off in, and land safely when flying conditions are not ideal. You want an airplane in which ordinary pilots can achieve extraordinary results.

Effective organizations want to develop a similar environment for the people who work there. They want an environment where ordinary employees can achieve extraordinary results. A practice field allows an organization to study and learn about its own enablers and potential disablers, in addition to learning about and enhancing the capabilities of its employees.

For example, consider a business director who is trying to develop a plan for increasing the profits of her product line. She has decided to call a meeting of the sales manager, the union representative, the human resources manager, and the manufacturing manager. The director is using a process of learning from the future to help the participants think through their own mental models and examine the mental models of the other attendees. Her desired outcome is to develop a robust set of strategic options that the group can support. She wants to be able to create an atmosphere that allows each person present to feel safe enough to bring down mental model barriers and listen as objectively as possible.

Learning From the Future

Outline

Step I: Identify the key issues or areas of concern (see Table 2).

1. State the objective of the exercise.
2. Develop a framing question that you want the exercise to answer.
3. Brainstorm a list of the critical issues related to the framing question.
4. Develop a list of a dozen or so critical issues.
5. Group the critical issues by common themes.
6. Give each grouping of the critical issues a descriptive name.

Table 2

> **Objective:** Develop a plan for increasing the profits of the
> product line
>
> > What are the critical issues involved in
> > reducing costs and increasing profits?
>
> **Operating Cost**   **The Market**   **Employees**
> •How do we control   •What is the market   •Employee apathy
> manufacturing costs? trend?   •Fear job security
> •How do we reduce   •What is the market •Union activities
> raw material costs? demand?

**Step II: Identify people who have a stake in resolving
this issue. Don't forget to include yourself on this list.
Develop a snapshot of the critical issues from the perspective of these stakeholders (see Table 3).**

1. Who has a stake in the outcome of this decision or issue?
2. What are his or her goals?
3. What is his or her current reality?
4. If his or her goals are achieved, what would success look
   like for this stakeholder?
5. What actions might this stakeholder take to move from
   current reality toward success?
6. What are this stakeholder's uncertainties relative to this
   issue?
   a. What are the barriers to the stakeholder's success?
   b. Are there events or conditions about which the stake-
      holder is unsure that could affect the ability to achieve
      his or her goal?

Table 3
Stakeholder Matrix

Key Players: Stakeholders or Systems	Goals	Description/ Measure of Current Reality	Measure of Success	Predisposition, Actions, or Strategies	Uncertainties Scenarios, Barriers
Manufactuuring Manager	Higher Q1 conversions	Conversions 10 percent below target	Conversions at 5 percent above target	—Fewer machine changes —Fewer products	—New budget constraints —Machine capability
Sales Manager	Greater return on sales	—Sold out —Unreliable supply	Meet volume demands	—Raise prices —Push mfg. harder	—Patience of board members —Competitor response
Human Resources Manager	Productive employees	Employee apathy, laziness	Employees stop griping	10 percent layoff —Lose dead weight	Union activites —Employees fear loss of job
Union	Maintain fair employment	Outsourcing rumors	—No outsourcing —Keep jobs	Strike	—Public support —Mngmnt. resolve —Global economy

Step III: Develop options for the stakeholders as individuals and as a group (see Figures 13 and 14).

1. Who are the key stakeholders?
2. Identify three or four strategic options these stakeholders might consider in order to achieve their goals. These options should not lie along the same line of action. They should, as much as possible, be diametrically opposed. Think out of the box.

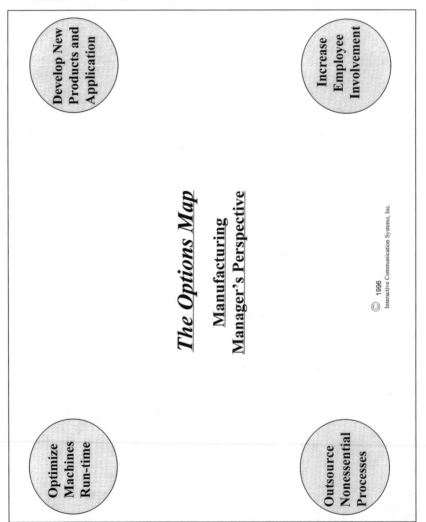

Figure 13

3. Define a range of three actions of stratregies around each option that could be exercised by the stakeholder.
4. Draw a line connecting the three or four actions or strategies that can be combined into a plausible, coherent strategy.
5. Repeat the exercise for each key stakeholder. Think of the group as a collective entity.

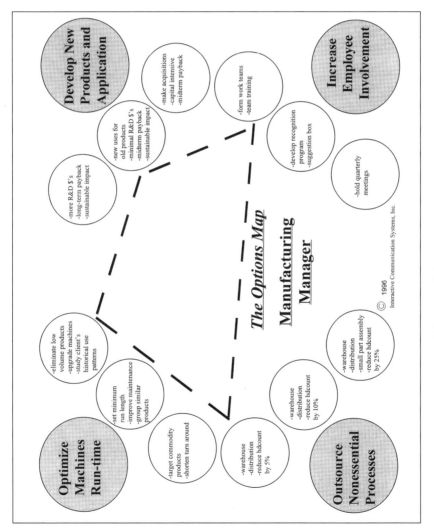

Figure 14

Step IV: Develop and identify the most resilient and robust strategy (see Table 4).

1. List the actions or strategic options selected from Step III in the "Strategies In" column on the left side of the matrix.
2. List the key uncertainties or barriers from Step II that are related to these options in the "Scenarios, Stories, or Uncertainties In" row across the top of the matrix.
3. If strategic option 1 is followed, and uncertainty or scenario 1 exists, answer the following questions and fill in the box below the scenario.
   a. What would you do?
   b. What would most likely happen?
   c. What strategy would you follow?
4. Follow the same process for each block of the matrix until the matrix is completed.
5. Write the answers to the following questions in the "Scenarios, Insights, Questions Out" row across the bottom of the matrix for each scenario.
   a. What insights did you gain by examining the strategies under each uncertainty or barrier?
   b. What new questions are raised from examining the strategies under each uncertainty or barrier?
6. Using the insights described above in number 5, rewrite the actions or strategies from the "Strategies In" column in the "Robust Strategies or Variables Out" column. Write them so that they are more robust and resilient with respect to what has been learned from the scenarios in the matrix.

Step V: Develop a causal loop diagram to describe the picture that has emerged (see Figure 15).

1. Develop the big picture for "what is"?
2. Develop the big picture of how the robust strategies take us to where we want to be.
3. Use causal loop diagrams to describe and test options.

Table 4

Scenario Matrix
Scenarios, Insights, Questions Out

Robust Strategies or Variables Out

Strategies In	Employees fear loss of jobs	No budget increase	Patience of board members	Robust Strategies or Variables Out
Outsource warehouse and distribution functions	—more errors —more complaints —lower profits	—lower spending and operating cost on paper —positive impact on profits	—quick bottom-line impact, on paper	Combine outsourcing with team processes and employee education
Develop new uses for existing products	—employees feel less threatened —greater employee commitment	—lower R&D cost —longer runs —incr. productivity	—quicker impact than new product development	—Eliminate low-volume products —Find new uses for remaining products
Form and train employee work teams	—employees share in the accountability —mentally engaged —opportunity to build synergy	—greater initial cost —lower long-term cost —greater productivity	—impact appears initially slow, but increases quickly	Develop employee accountability and synergy through team-based collaboration
—Use client order history to plan runs **—Eliminate low-volume products**	—concern for job security	—incr. planning efficiency —lower operating cost —longer runs	—increase machine utilization —quick impact	Increase efficiency with fewer machine changes
	Involving employees improves chances of outsourcing success	—bottom-line impact —Interrelated actions —No silver bullet	Communicate need for front-end patience	

The causal loop diagram should be a dynamic, living map. The map can be used to test how the new system will react to internal and external influences, in addition to providing a visual perception of the system.

The Continuous Improvement Process

If an organization is going to survive beyond its foreseeable future, it is essential that it learns how to recognize, assess, and appropriately respond to both internal and external changes. Success today does not guarantee success tomorrow. Competitors will change their strategies; customers will develop different needs; new technology will continue to emerge. All these changes make it necessary for each organization to continue to improve the products and services being offered if it is to remain competitive as the market evolves. Organizations are much like organisms: if they are unable to adapt, they are destined to extinction.

Organizations generally form around a recognized mar-

Figure 15
Causal Loop Diagram of the Robust Strategy

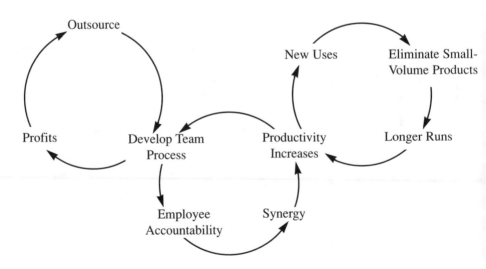

ket opportunity or need. They focus on their identified ability to meet that need as a substitute for their competitors' products and services, as a compliment to those products and services, or to fill a niche that their competitors have not chosen or are unable to address. The matrix in Figure 16 shows the four areas where companies typically perform: doing the right things well, the right things poorly, the wrong things well, or the wrong things poorly.

Figure 16
Organizational Performance Matrix

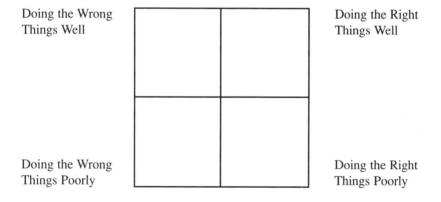

Doing the Wrong Things Well

Doing the Right Things Well

Doing the Wrong Things Poorly

Doing the Right Things Poorly

Each company, regardless of its market, wants to perform, doing the right things well (see Figure 17). Before a company is able to do this, however, it may initially provide a desired product or service that it is unable to produce effectively and efficiently. It may be doing the right things, but it may be doing the right things poorly (see Figure 18).

With some effort and investment in time and money, the company gradually finds ways to improve quality, reduce costs, reduce overhead, and improve efficiencies. As the organization develops and implements methods and systems to improve internal and external processes for providing

Figure 17
Where organizations want to operate

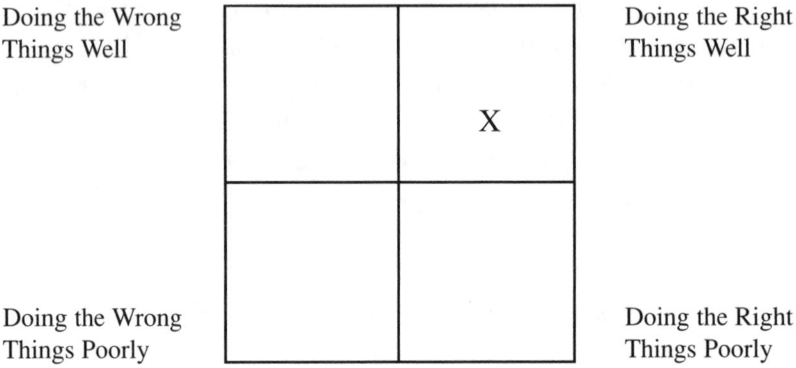

Doing the Wrong Things Well		Doing the Right Things Well
	X	
Doing the Wrong Things Poorly		Doing the Right Things Poorly

"X" marks the region in which every organization wants to perform.

Figure 18
Where organizations typically begin operating

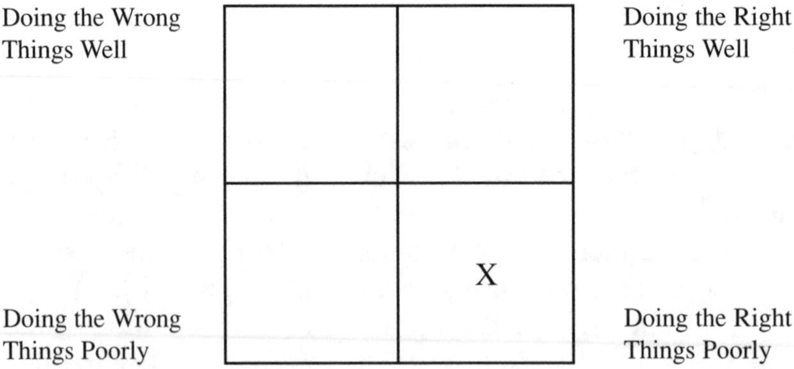

Doing the Wrong Things Well		Doing the Right Things Well
Doing the Wrong Things Poorly	X	Doing the Right Things Poorly

When most organizations are just getting started, they know what the right things are, but they are not experienced at doing them well.

Figure 19

*Practice and applied learning sharpen the skills needed to
move an organization to doing the right things well*

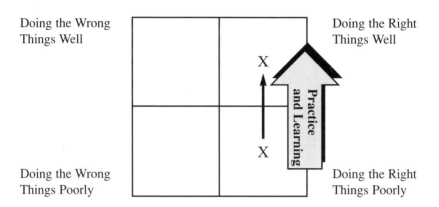

products and services, it begins to move from doing the
right things poorly to doing the right things well. The
process that moves an organization from doing the right
things poorly to doing the right things well is called **practice**. The applied process that helps to keep it in that quadrant is called **learning** (see Figure 19).

As technology changes, along with the drivers that influence the market and the needs of the customer base, the
company may find that the products and services it is providing no longer meet the customers' needs. The company
discovers that instead of producing the right things well, it
is now producing the wrong things well (see Figure 20).

This scenario is played out over and over again in sports
like basketball and football. In these sports, it often happens
that during the first half of play, one team (let's call them
the red team) builds what appears to be an insurmountable
lead over their opponents (let's call them the blue team). It

Figure 20

The direction in which many organizations tend to move

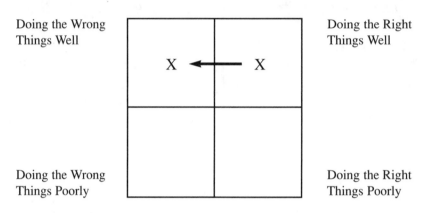

Doing the Wrong Things Well	Doing the Right Things Well
Doing the Wrong Things Poorly	Doing the Right Things Poorly

> **Changing market conditions or customer needs may cause an organzation's products and services to become obsolete.**

---

seems that the red team has developed and is executing a strategy that will put them in the winner's circle. They are a team that has defined what the right thing is, and is apparently doing it well.

The blue team enters the locker room at halftime. The players realize that if they are going to have any chance at winning the game, they must make some adjustments in their strategy. They realize that they have been doing the wrong things. Through the assessment of their coaches, the statistician, and others, they devise a strategy to counteract the strategy of the red team.

When the two teams come back on the playing field to begin the second half, the blue team starts to execute their adjusted strategy. If they are successful, and if the red team continues to use the same strategy they used in the first half, the red team may find their lead start to dwindle. The red team may be executing their original strategy perfectly, but the adjustments in the strategy of the blue team have made the red team's strategy less effective. Whereas the red team was once doing the right things well, they find that they are now doing the wrong things well.

It is important to understand that the skills of the red team have not changed, their personnel is the same, the arena is the same, their execution is the same. However, the action taken by the blue team has changed, and caused the red team to move from doing the right things well to doing the wrong things well. If the red team is unable to adjust to the blue team's new strategy, the game will be lost.

IBM played out a similar scenario in the 1970s and 1980s. It developed and implemented a strategy to supply a growing computer industry with mainframe computers. It described the typical customer as a large company with enough money to invest in a mainframe system, and supply employees with "dummy" terminals that were useful only as long as they were tied in to the mainframe. Every person with a dummy terminal had access only to the software that was available on the mainframe computer. With one of the best and most respected names in the industry, IBM developed a system of service and hardware that clearly established it as the leader in the computer industry. It looked as though its position in the market was unchallengeable. IBM had clearly defined a game, and a strategy for playing that game, and it was doing the right things very well.

However, in 1984, Steven Jobs of Apple Computer decided to create a new paradigm, making new rules for what a computer should be and who the customer might be. By developing and successfully marketing the personal computer, Jobs offered individuality to a person's computer needs. No longer was a user limited to the software that was available on the mainframe. The personal computer became a tool that the average middle-class family could afford. This took computers out of government and corporate offices. They became accessible to classrooms, homes, churches, and small businesses. This opened a whole new market for business and educational software. These moves were so successful that other hardware manufacturers began to spring up, and to develop and implement similar strategies.

As a result of moves by Apple and others, IBM saw the profits from mainframe computers begin to decline. It was still as efficient as before. Its service was as good as ever, but, because of a new paradigm, the market for computers had changed. Finally, in the mid-1980s, IBM realized that if it was going to successfully compete, it would have to change its strategy. It would have to find new right things, and learn how to do them well.

The PC junior was IBM's first entrée into this new market paradigm. This was its new "right things." After some months, however, it became clear that in several specifications, the PC junior did not perform at the level of many of the competitors' models. The market and customer reaction taught IBM that it needed to move in the direction of the personal computer. IBM applied its technology to defining and developing new right things. Unfortunately, at this stage, it was doing the right things, but poorly.

Over the past decade or so, IBM has continued to apply its learning and to practice its core skills. It has been able to apply these to the development of new technology, processes, and hardware. As a result, IBM has moved back up into the "doing the right things well" quadrant. It is clear, however, that unless practice and applied learning continue, there is no guarantee that it will remain there.

It is often a shock to organizations, which at one time enjoyed some level of success, to find their earnings and measures of customer satisfaction beginning to slip. They rationalize that they are still performing the same functions efficiently. They wonder why those functions, while still efficient, now seem less effective. They fail to understand that it is not always necessary for a company's process efficiency to deteriorate in order for performance, especially as it relates to customer satisfaction, to decline. Many organizations move from doing the right things well to doing the wrong things well while maintaining the same levels of efficiency.

The move to doing the wrong things well may, in fact, not be caused by anything internal to the organization. The shift may instead be triggered by external forces, like new technologies, moves by competitors, or the changing needs of the customer. Any of these forces may result in loss of market share and lower revenues.

The transition from doing the right things well to doing the wrong things well can occur in virtually any organization. The only question is, How quickly does it occur? In the automobile industry, this transition occurs in approximately twelve-month intervals with the introduction of the new model year. In the fast-paced world of software and computers, the transition occurs approximately every thirty days. The surest way for a company to lose ground in any industry is to keep doing what it's doing, continuing to produce to yesterday's standards. If businesses don't learn how to make the necessary adjustments, they are likely to have a very short life.

Of course, the logical step for any company to take is to determine how to move from doing the wrong things well back to doing the new right things well. What most organizations fail to understand, however, is that once they determine what the new right things are, it is nearly impossible to move directly from doing the wrong things well to doing the new right things well. The transition that most often occurs is one that moves the organization from doing the wrong things well to doing the new right things poorly (see Figure 21). The process of transitioning an organization from doing the wrong things to identifying and doing the right things is called **coaching** (see Figure 22). The impact of coaching on the culture of the organization is called **change** (see Figure 23).

Figure 21
Initial impact of continuous improvement process

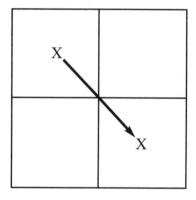

Doing the Wrong Things Well

Doing the Right Things Well

Doing the Wrong Things Poorly

Doing the Right Things Poorly

> **Because it is new to an organization, the first step in the continuous improvement process is to do the right things poorly.**

Figure 22
The role of coaching

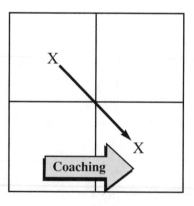

Doing the Wrong Things Well

Doing the Right Things Well

Doing the Wrong Things Poorly

Doing the Right Things Poorly

> **Coaching is the method by which new skills are communicated, designed to move an organization in the direction of desired performance.**

Figure 23
Organizational change

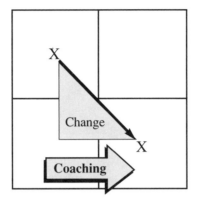

Doing the Wrong Things Well

Doing the Right Things Well

Doing the Wrong Things Poorly

Doing the Right Things Poorly

Change

Coaching

X

X

Organizational change occurs when a new process is introduced, designed to bring a company back to where it wants to operate.

These steps are common to nearly all learning processes. The degree to which the wrong things are ingrained in the culture will determine magnitude of the change as well as the impact of that change on the lives of employees.

For example, crawling is a natural stage of development that children experience before they begin to walk. They really get pretty good at quickly moving around on their hands and knees, going wherever their curiosity leads them.

Somewhere around eight or nine months of age, however, children begin to discover and explore the skill of walking as a more powerful mode of transportation. But before they begin to walk, they first experiment with standing. The first attempts to stand find the child on wobbly legs. With any luck, they may be able to hold that position for several seconds before losing their balance and tumbling to the ground, landing on a well-padded bottom. Finally, after some practice, junior stands more confidently. He dares to test those new leg muscles, and lunges forward in that first frightening, yet exciting, uncontrollable step.

Did the child take a step? Yes, but not very well. The parents are usually so excited about this accomplishment, however, that they tell Grandma, the uncles and aunts, and all the neighbors about this newsworthy event. Junior, of course, thinks all this attention is really cool. Because recognition encourages more of the same behavior, junior decides to repeat this daring feat.

At some point, the child begins to experiment by putting these wobbly steps together, and starts to execute what we call walking. But let's face it. At this stage of development, junior is not going to win a gold medal for his performance. He is walking, but he is not walking very well. He is doing the right thing, but he is doing it poorly. In order to do the right thing well, junior must continue to practice those wobbly walking skills. He must learn how to balance and coordinate those newly discovered muscles. Everyone knows that junior must begin by doing the right things poorly if he is ever going to learn how to do the right things well. It is when he is doing the right things poorly that he most needs patience and recognition from his parents.

Organizations often fail to anticipate that they will probably not transition directly to doing the right things well. They often do not realize that the first steps in doing the right things well usually begin with doing the right things poorly. They don't anticipate the role of the learning process. They may have sold this new right things idea to upper management, and now upper management is breathing down their necks, anxious for them to produce the promised bottom-line results. They get nervous.

Like the child taking his first steps, doing the right things poorly may be interesting and exciting. However, because people in other parts of the organization are using different measures of success, doing the right things poorly may not be a particularly comfortable place for the team to exist. It is for this reason that patience and recognition for successful "baby steps" by the team in the new process are so important. These encourage employees to continue embracing the learning process in which they are involved.

Doing the right things, because it is new and different, and represents significant change, can be frightening and challenging. It is important at this stage that employees know that the company is committed to the process of learning how to do the right things well, however long it takes to get there.

Because the full benefits are not immediately observed, it is often at this point that many organizations begin to slip back into the old, comfortable ways of doing things. It doesn't matter that they are doing the wrong things again. It's comfortable. They may reason that in the short term, the bottom line doesn't show it costing as much as implementing the right things. After all, this is what employees are already trained to do. On this basis, some organizations may even choose to entirely abandon their attempts to learn how to do the new right things well.

What the organization is wrestling with is the culture change that is required to move from doing the wrong things well to doing the right things poorly. The magnitude and the impact of that change will be largely determined by the extent to which doing the wrong things is ingrained in the organizational culture.

Let's suppose a child comes to a third-grade math class to study the multiplication tables. If that child tells the teacher that 3 x 3 = 10, the child will be corrected immediately and told that 3 x 3 = 9. The child can put this correction in his or her memory bank with relative ease, and begin using it almost immediately.

Let's suppose that the teacher does not immediately correct the student, and allows the student to practice this false mathematical relationship for thirty-five years before correcting the mistake. In this instance, it would be much more difficult after thirty-five years for the student to replace the practiced belief that 3 x 3 = 10 with 3 x 3 = 9. Because the student has now been practicing the false relationship for thirty-five years, making the change to the right relationship represents a much greater change than learning the correct relationship in the third-grade math class.

A similar occurrence is observed when a person decides that he or she wants to learn to play the game of golf. Playing golf involves more than just hitting the ball. It involves the proper grip on the club, the proper head position, the proper stance, the right rhythm, and so. To the beginner, these behaviors feel awkward and unnatural. With practice and instruction, however, all of these factors come together in what is called muscle memory. The beginner approaches the game with bad habits and mistaken notions about what it means to swing a golf club. If these habits are not corrected early in the learning process, the person may be able to play the game, but he or she will probably always play the game poorly, doing the wrong things well. A person who is learning to play golf is always advised to take lessons early in the learning process, because it is always easier to coach a person to play the game the right way before he or she has mastered playing the game the wrong way.

The longer and more proficiently an organization has been doing the wrong things well, the greater the magnitude of change when it tries to begin doing the right things. It's not impossible to teach an old dog new tricks, but you must be patient and persistent enough to allow the change to take hold.

Of course, it is sometimes the case that a company finds that it has moved into the quadrant of doing the wrong things poorly. This move can occur anyplace on the chart (see Figure 23). This kind of change often occurs as the result of the threat of layoffs, an expected reorganization, a loss of focus, or senior management's failure to engage employees in a strong sense of purpose. The result is often confusion and

Figure 24

Organizations sometimes find themselves operating here

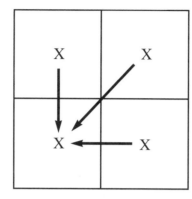

Doing the Wrong Things Well	Doing the Right Things Well
Doing the Wrong Things Poorly	Doing the Right Things Poorly

> **A loss of focus and low morale are among the primary reasons
> an organization begins to do the wrong things poorly.**

low employee morale. There is a growing preoccupation with job security, which distracts from the attention that needs to be given to current roles and responsibilities.

When this occurs, senior management must quickly establish a clear vision, articulating it to employees. Employees must be mentally engaged, feeling a shared responsibility with the management team for achieving the vision. They need to understand why the course has been set. Management must communicate what kind of commitment it will take to reach the new goals, and what the consequences are to the company if the new objectives are not achieved. If this is not done, the company may soon find itself being destroyed from the inside out. Its biggest barrier may be its employees and its organizational processes.

When making these transitions, individuals and organizations need to remember two things:

1. It is impossible to move from doing the wrong things to doing the right things without some significant change

occurring. The magnitude of that change will be different from individual to individual, from organization to organization, and from transition to transition. It will, however, always be present at some significant, emotional level. Help employees who will be responsible for learning and practicing the new process to develop some awareness and appreciation for the magnitude of the change, before trying to coach them in doing the new right things.

2. Regardless of when the transition to the right things begins, the individual and the organization must remember to exercise patience and persistence during the critical learning phase. Although some positive effect may occur on the bottom line during various stages of learning, the full benefit of doing the right things will probably not be seen on the bottom line until the learning process is well under way. Let the organization know, up front, that this may take some time. It may be helpful to develop a learning timeline as well as a success timeline to keep the organization informed of the progress as it occurs.

6

The Fire Fighting Paradox

When high-performance teams are observed, five critical success factors routinely appear. The degree to which these factors are present will largely determine to what degree the team is successful. These critical success factors are as follows:

1. The team must consist of people who are mentally engaged and committed to the goal.
2. The individual team members must be committed to the success of other team members.
3. The team must share a common experience base.
4. The team must establish goals that are engaging and have personal significance.
5. The team spends more time on the practice field than on the playing field.

This chapter examines these critical success factors as they relate to real-life fire fighting by a high-performance team and to fire fighting that occurs within an organization.

I have always found it interesting that terms commonly associated with fire are generally used in a negative sense to describe the high-level, intense, focused, but often nonsystemic activities that occur in an organization during a crisis.

Organizations use the term "burning platform" to describe an issue or set of circumstances that raises the sense of urgency of a group to a level where it is compelled to act. The term apparently had its origins in the oil industry, where drilling platforms are erected in the ocean many miles from shore. Men and women live and work on these drilling platforms for extended periods. The drilling platform represents safety and security in the middle of a vast sea of seen and unseen dangers. Every precaution is taken to make the people working there comfortable, productive, and safe.

Occasionally, however, in spite of the care that is taken to protect the lives of these men and women, something goes wrong. A fire breaks out. The precious crude oil, which represents billions of dollars to the company that owns the drilling platform, suddenly becomes the deadly fuel that feeds the fire. What was to be the source of income and financial stability for those on the drilling platform now becomes the agent of mass destruction. They fight to save the drilling platform, and they fight to save their own lives.

If the fire reaches the point where the inhabitants of the drilling platform realize that they have lost control, they find themselves faced with a decision that is critical to their survival. They have to decide whether to stay on the drilling platform and be consumed, or to jump into the frigid waters of the sea and risk survival among unknown dangers. When the situation reaches this critical point, they quickly realize that the odds of survival are greater among the unknown risks of the sea than they are on the burning drilling platform. They are left, then, with only one logical course of action: to jump into the sea.

Many organizations, needing to implement changes in their operations, must first find themselves in an emergency situation, faced with the threat of significant loss, before they are willing to make a move. It takes a burning platform experience to motivate them to make crucial changes. The burning platform may take the form of a competitive threat, an unexpected change in technology, the loss of a critical customer to the competition, a shift in the economy, or any number of things that could have been anticipated, but whose warning signs were ignored.

Perhaps the phrase that organizations use most to describe the mode they enter to resolve unexpected issues is "fire fighting." Fire fighting means that the people in an organization find it difficult to routinely rally around any existing goal or vision. They rarely show any real cohesiveness of spirit until an emergency arises. Emergencies often take the form of an excursion in quality, a complaint or a product return from an important customer, or a sudden decline in productivity. Any incident that unexpectedly and significantly threatens the earnings, external image, or survival of an organization is commonly called a fire.

In the fire fighting mode, even poor organizations often look good. A fire gives the organization's leadership and employees a common threat around which to rally. A fire makes it necessary to set clear goals and objectives that mentally engage every employee. Like soldiers in basic training, everyone has the opportunity for a common experience base, from which a new behavior can be forged.

Fires caused by natural processes, such as lightning, may add great value in helping to maintain the delicate balance of nature. There are some plants, like the giant redwood trees of California, that need this kind of trauma to release their seedlings and survive. In organizations, however, this is rarely the case. While unexpected flare-ups of the kind we are talking about here may spur an organization to recognize and correct a previously unnoticed deficiency, their occurrence is typically indicative of an organization whose goals and objectives are unclear, and whose employees are not mentally engaged in accomplishing those goals. An organization that can only engage its employees around flare-ups is operating dangerously, and is subjecting itself to a wasteful drain on capital and human resources.

To further complicate the situation, many organizations openly reward employees who appear to be fire fighting heroes. Employees, who want to get positive recognition from the organization, learn and understand this process. As a result, fires break out from time to time, drawing a lot of attention and praise to the fire fighters, while the departments or individuals who are trying to practice fire prevention go virtually unnoticed.

To gain some insight into the concept of "fire fighting" and how its principles relate to business processes, I spent some time with a group of experts. I scheduled some time to talk with and observe a class of twenty-two recruits from the training academy of the Charlotte Fire Department (CFD), in Charlotte, North Carolina. Captain Jerry Rodgers and his class of recruits were kind enough to allow me to observe and participate in two live burns. Let's look at the role of the five critical success factors in this team.

Critical Success Factor #1

The team must consist of people who are mentally engaged and committed to the goal.

Unlike other groups, the fire department has no regular class schedule for training new fire fighters. The turnover is typically very low, and it is common for fire fighters to remain in the department for twenty-five or more years. New classes are started only on an as-needed basis, often as the result of municipal annexation or to replace retirees.

The application process takes about a year, and includes

a written test, a lie detector test, an in-depth background check, and grueling, physical fitness requirements. The irregular class schedule, along with these stringent requirements, indicates how uncertain it is that an applicant will be accepted into the program. There were members of this particular class who had been applying to the program for as long as eleven years. Once accepted in the program, only the very best will be able to sustain the performance necessary to successfully complete the training.

As in many organizations, when these twenty-two recruits came together for the first time in February of that year, they were complete strangers. It was the job of Captain Rodgers and his team of instructors to build this group into a cohesive, high-performance team by the end of June. By the time I met this class, they had been practicing the values and principles involved in working together as a team for five months. They had come to believe that these concepts are more than just theory, but that they are critical to the life and safety of each individual and, ultimately, to the entire team of fire fighters.

Critical Success Factor #2

The individual team members must be committed to the success of other team members.

In my interviews with the recruits, I was curious how they felt about working in a team-based environment. I also wondered if there was a defining experience where they stopped performing as individuals and started to gel as a team. I was surprised at how easy it was for the recruits to recall what they believed the turning point to be.

It seems that part of their training involved donning full gear and crawling through an eighty-foot section of pipe that was eighteen inches in diameter and buried five feet underground. While this sounds like a relatively simple exercise, being in total darkness, in very close quarters, while being weighed down with fifteen to twenty pounds of clothing and gear, including an air pack strapped to your back, and having your face covered by a full face mask is a frightening, claustrophobic experience. This experience threatened to unnerve several of the recruits.

What the recruits described as the factor that contributed most to their success during this exercise was the verbal encouragement from their fellow recruits. While trying to squeeze through that dark section of pipe, the recruits described being able to feel the sides of that pipe close in around them. They couldn't see anything in front of them or behind them, but they could hear their teammates cheering them on and encouraging them to make it through. Every person who made it through that pipe was successful because of the help and support of fellow team members. One of the defining qualities of a high-performance team is that each member is interested in and encourages the success of the other team members. Every person on the team now knew without a doubt that he or she could depend on that kind of support as a result of their own experience together.

Critical Success Factor #3
The team must share a common experience base.

This exercise gave them a common experience base on which to build their core values. They learned what it means to be able to depend on each other. It gave them something they could all talk about, reflect on, and understand. They could all relate to each other's fear of possible failure and hope for ultimate success as a result of this common experience base. After this, nothing could shake their confidence in each other.

After the common experience base had been established, it was easy to hear stories circulating among the class indicating that the team had begun to gel.

My favorite is the one about the recruit who was, for a long time, unsuccessful in completing his mile and a half run within the specified time. He missed getting an exceptional on his physical fitness test, because he was five seconds too slow in the mile and a half run. He was given two days to meet the physical fitness requirements, or he would be expelled from the program. His team members were determined that he was not going to fail, so they all got together on the morning of his retest, and paced him through the run. As they ran, they talked with him, they encouraged him, and they urged him on. When the mile and a half was completed, the recruit, with the help of his teammates, had shaved thirty-five seconds off his previous best time.

All these experiences would prove to be critical to their success during the last few days of training. These were special days. It was during these days that the live burns occurred. It would be the first time that the class would experience fire fighting in a burning structure. These were the days where all the skills and principles they had learned over the previous five months about teamwork would finally come together in a potentially life-threatening training situation.

The live burn consisted of finding a structure or building that was slated for demolition, and using that structure to create a live house fire scenario. The house would be burned from back to front, using diesel fuel as the propellant for the fire. If this were a real fire, a hole would be cut into the roof of the structure to allow the hot gases to vent to the outside. For training purposes, however, the instructors wanted to create a worse-case scenario. For this reason, a hole was not cut into the roof. This created an environment that pushed the temperatures inside the burning structure up as high as 1200°F.

An instructor was stationed in one doorway of the burning room so that he could observe the performance of the teams of recruits as they entered the room through another doorway to knock down the fire. When one team of recruits had successfully completed their task, the fire was reignited, and another team of recruits was sent in. This rotation continued until the building was no longer safe to enter and was destroyed.

The recruits assembled themselves in teams of four. The lead person was assigned the role of operating the nozzle. That person was primarily responsible for getting the fire under control. The three other team members positioned themselves behind the lead person along the length of fire hose. It was their role to help maneuver the hose into and out of the building.

Fire fighters are taught that the fire hose is their lifeline. If you can find the hose, you can always find your way out of a burning building. I learned firsthand how important that principle is as I was given the opportunity to put on the gear of a fire fighter and be the lead person.

My team and I crawled into the room which by now was engulfed in flames. The flames were only a couple of feet above the floor. As instructed by Captain Rodgers, I lay on my left side and opened the nozzle on the fire hose full, pointing it toward the ceiling. I was told to do a circular spray pattern on the ceiling and then to hit the base of the fire with the spray of water. When I did this, it became immediately apparent why working as a team is so critical. As soon as the water extinguished the fire, the room filled with black, suffocating smoke. The room instantly had zero visibility. My only sense of connectedness and encouragement came from my team members behind me, as I felt them tug on the fire hose, maneuvering it to make it easier for me to do my job.

Because of the extreme temperatures, the water that had been sprayed on the flames was immediately converted to steam. The pressure and the moist heat from the steam, along with the lack of visibility caused by dense smoke, created a feeling of disorientation. I realized that finding my way out of the room would be difficult. In addition, the person operating the nozzle is taught never to turn his or her back on the fire. When I shouted the signal, indicating that it was safe to crawl back out of the room, I had to rely on the members of my team to gently lead me out, using the hose as a guide. The feel of my team members tugging on the hose was my only feeling of security. They trusted me to take care of knocking down the fire. I trusted them to lead me safely out of the building. As long as I could feel that tug, I felt certain that everything was all right.

Critical Success Factor #4

The team must establish goals that are engaging and have personal significance.

In several follow-up discussions, I spoke with some of the men who had been part of my team. I asked whether fire fighters set any particular goals for themselves and for their team. I was told that there are two primary goals. The first surprising but, in retrospect, obvious goal is to prevent fires. Fire fighters are happiest when they have no fires to fight. They don't mind spending time in schools and with civic groups, helping people understand the dangers associated with fires, in hopes of raising the awareness of the community they serve. As a result, the goal is not to fight fires, but to help the community find ways to keep fires from occurring.

The second goal is even more important than the first: to come home alive. In fire prevention, if the first line of defense is breached, this second goal becomes the primary goal. It requires the unselfish efforts of every person on the team looking out for every other person on the team to ensure that the second goal is accomplished every day.

Critical Success Factor #5

The team spends more time on the practice field than on the playing field.

One of the critical lessons from this experience is that high-performance teams always spend more time on the practice field than they do on the playing field. The elements of what make a team great are found in the philosophy and quality of their practice, not in the nuances of their organization.

When an organization decides to use team-based processes to accomplish its objectives, many groups begin by bringing in an internal or external human resources guru, who spends most of his or her time helping the organization's leadership define the goal and the hierarchical reporting relationships of the team. The second step commonly taken by the organization's leadership and the HR guru is to spend considerable time discussing the structure and make-up of the team. When this is completed, the team is called together, given its charge, and sent off to fight its designated fire. Surprisingly, it is often the case that little or no provision is made for the team to practice the skills needed to fight fires. When the practice field is absent, there are generally several outcomes:

1. **Virtually every role performed by the team is executed in real time.** While it is certainly admirable to be able to act and react in real time, it is not easy to sustain this level of activity. This makes it difficult at best to improve on skills when the only opportunity to develop those skills occurs during the game.

2. **Because the window of opportunity for learning is limited, there is little or no time to assess or expand the capacity of the team to achieve its goals.** When the team's opportunity for learning is limited, the team's capacity to succeed or to handle more difficult challenges may never be fully realized.

3. **There is no opportunity for continuous improvement of existing processes.** The team continues to operate using the methods that were successful in fighting yesterday's fires. Team members may find themselves incapable of addressing the emerging, unexpected, internal and external challenges of tomorrow.

4. **There is little opportunity for shared learning.** When the fire is raging, the team must be decisive. The team members know their roles, and the team depends on each member to perform his or her role. There is little time for shared learning or analysis. The best learning takes place on the practice field, where the risks are relatively low, and sharing and reflection are encouraged.

   For fire fighters in the Charlotte Fire Department, practice begins in the station house. They routinely familiarize themselves with the layout of buildings and structures in the area. They also review any extenuating factors that might exist, like low water pressure in certain neighborhoods or how a certain structure should be approached. By doing this, fire fighters create a mental practice field. For them, this is where anticipatory learning occurs. In addition, fire fighters spend at least two days a month practicing the skills of fire fighting and EMT at the academy.

5. **There is little or no opportunity to discover and develop ways of preventing fires.** There is much to be learned about fire prevention as investigators sift through the rubble of a home that has been destroyed by fire. These lessons are important, but it should never be necessary to burn down a house in order to learn the right lessons. When the fire is fully engaged, fire fighters must dedicate their time and attention to fighting the fire. Strategies for fire prevention are developed before the fire. Fire prevention at its best is an outgrowth of applied practice field experiences.

Effective fire prevention processes are learned during practice. While knowing how to fight fires effectively is a critical survival skill, fire fighting is not the goal. Fire fighting is actually the last line of defense. The primary goal, and the first line of defense, is fire prevention. Fire fighters try to anticipate that potential, and work to educate their clients in such a way as to avoid that potential. In the event, however, that that potential does arrive, the skills are there to address it.

In spite of our best efforts, in any organization there will be fires from time to time. This is the reality of doing business. Flare-ups occur because no organization, even with the best strategic planning tools, can perfectly predict or envision its competitive future. While practice fields are important, they are not perfect. What an organization learns from envisioning the future will always be flawed, but trying to stay competitive without having a practice field in which to explore that future is like weightlifting without first trying to build up muscle: you may survive for a while, but your competitors will soon surpass you.

Through practice, high-performance teams learn how to anticipate the future, learn from it, and plan for it. Yes, fire fighting is often exciting, and it sometimes spawns the occasional, promotable hero. It is absolutely essential, however, to the long-term success of any organization to learn how to recognize, encourage, and reward fire prevention. The organization that rewards prevention will usually get better at prevention.

7

The Bcube™ Process: Studies and Observations

Hundreds of people in corporate groups, small businesses, and training, educational, and civic organizations have experienced the Bcube™ process. Let's look at some team and individual participation and learning behaviors that have been observed.

Recognition

At some point in the series of exercises, each group begins to spontaneously recognize itself for accomplishing its tasks. It is interesting to note just how far into the exercises each group goes before it begins to do this. Some groups do this from the very first exercise, while other groups begin much later. Eventually, however, every group engages in some form of self-recognition, whether it be with cheers, high fives, or applause. They begin to realize that recognition is a natural response, driven by people internal to the team. It is driven by people who know the value of their accomplishments and the contributions of each person on the team to achieving the team's success.

Recognition cannot have its roots in a formalized program that is external to the team. The team wants to know that it has made a positive impact on the bottom line. As a result, the most significant and sincere recognition comes from those who were there when it happened: the team members themselves. Moreover, it is critical that teams be given time to celebrate successes, even small ones.

I have observed in every workshop setting that meaningful recognition is derived from a natural response to effective teamwork, not from a corporate-driven initiative. While some form of corporate-sponsored recognition is important, the team must drive and initiate the recognition process at a grassroots level in order to maximize its sincerity and effectiveness. The corporate program functions as a framework, establishing recognition as a corporate value. The corporate program does not function as the driver.

During the early stages of the Bcube™ process, I thought about asking the teams to recognize their accomplishments in the early exercises. I decided instead to wait and see how long it would take for recognition to naturally emerge from the team's feeling of mutual accomplishment and trust. Consequently, this has become an unofficial barometer of the degree to which true teamwork is occurring.

Naming the Game

In the "Naming the Game" exercise, a game is described that sounds like football, golf, soccer, or some other familiar team sport. The participants are assembled in teams of four to seven people. They are given an objective, and are asked to develop a strategy for accomplishing that objective. After the strategy has been developed, the teams post their work on a flipchart and make oral presentations to the larger group.

As the teams undertake this task, they mentally and verbally go through a process in which they try to fit the objective to a game structure that is familiar to them. Once the team decides on a likely structure for the game, they proceed to develop a strategy that conforms to the rules of that game.

If there are members of the team who are not familiar with the agreed-upon game structure, they typically contribute few ideas, allowing their more "knowledgeable" team members to develop the bulk of the strategy. This is often observed in seminars in the United States, when the teams consist of males and females and the described game structure sounds like a football game. In this example, the women who are not familiar with the game quickly admit their lack of knowledge; the men then proceed to lead the strategy-building exercise. The strategies they develop and present to the larger group indeed look very much like a page from the playbook of an NFL team (see Figures 25 and 26).

Figure 25
Examples of Output from the
"Naming of the Game" Exercise

Team 1 Output

- At the scrimmage line, seven of our team members will be dressed in thong bikinis and stiletto heels to deflect attention from the quarterback.

- Our best runner, Pam, will be dressed in an old flannel nightgown, fuzzy slippers, and rolled-down stockings. She will also wear pink sponge rollers.

> Notice how team 1 tried to be outrageous in their strategy, but evidence of the mental model of a football game is still clearly seen in the terminology used in the description.

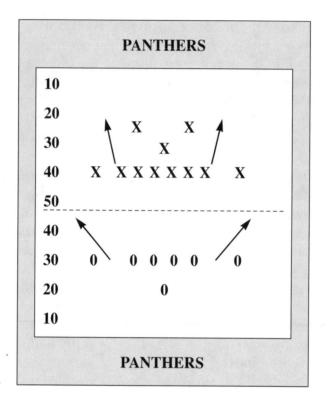

Figure 26
Team 2 Output

This exercise is a good way to get the participants to interact around a simple objective that has no right or wrong answers. It allows the facilitator to get the first glimpse into the dynamics of the team interaction, leadership, level of trust, and listening skills. Teams discover that the way they approach this exercise mirrors the way they interact around the conference room table in their real-work environment.

For example, one team found it difficult to raise and resolve conflict. One of the team members, trying to get the discussion in the "Naming the Game" exercise started, decided to break the ice by making what she intended to be a ridiculous joke. In this case, the objective sounded like a version of football. She suggested that the best strategy should involve using wheelchairs to accomplish the team objective. The rest of the team immediately accepted the suggestion as real, and developed a strategy that included wheelchairs. This member later revealed how incredulous and frustrated she was that her team was so unwilling to question something that was, she thought, so blatantly silly. Rather than risk raising and resolving the conflict, the team was willing to develop a strategy out of the ridiculous.

On the flip side, this team member who originally made the suggestion could have stopped the tangential team discussion, but she did not feel that the working environment with her colleagues was open and trusting enough to speak up again. As a result, she was not willing to stop the free-fall discussion by letting the team members know that her suggestion was only made in jest. In the end, the team developed a strategy that nobody liked, but that no one would criticize.

During the debrief, the team began to see how this scenario often plays itself out during their day-to-day interactions. Here is a clear example of how the team behaviors that exist in the workplace day to day are brought to this practice field and continue to operate in these simple exercises. If feelings like the ones described here can surface so strongly around a simple exercise that has minimal consequences, how much more intensely and tragically do they occur when critical issues about real situations and real people are being debated?

Because these scenarios around communication and trust continue to play out during the subsequent exercises, the facilitator does not need to expose these issues too vigorously at this point in the process. The facilitator can strategically discuss them in more depth as the participants experience these principles in the later exercises.

In the "Naming the Game" exercise, the participants discover that they cannot define a strategy for accomplishing their objective without first making some assumptions about the nature of the game. They consciously and unconsciously fit the stated objective to a preexisting mental model. If that mental model is football, the team develops a strategy that looks very much like a football game. If that mental model is hockey, then the team develops a strategy that looks very much like a hockey game.

To develop a successful, comprehensive strategy, the team must begin by defining the nature and boundaries of the game. In so doing, however, the team members learn that as soon as they define these boundaries or give the game a name, they immediately impose rules on themselves by which they will play the game and define their strategy. In addition to imposing rules on themselves, they also impose rules by which they believe their competitors will play the game. An effective, robust strategy is developed when the team does not define the game too early or the rules of the game too rigidly.

These same principles apply to any organization or company that is in the process of developing a strategy. It begins by gathering market intelligence about the customers, the competitors, the size and growth rate of the market, and so on. These data are then used to develop certain assumptions about the customer base, the market, and the "rules" by which competitors will likely play in that market. The organization then assesses its own capabilities and core competencies. Based on these inputs, the company decides whether and how it will play the game.

The need to think out of the box during the strategy development stage is critical. If an organization defines its strategy too rigidly, the inevitable midcourse corrections will feel more like a major reorganization. The organization runs the risk of moving its operations into the doing the wrong things poorly quadrant, having to wrestle with all the issues that accompany such a move.

Effective strategies, developed by groups that are able to

think out of the box, are able to adjust to the changing rules of the game. The FASTBreak™ process described in Chapter 5 is an effective tool for building flexibility and robustness into a strategy.

Every organization must routinely assess whether the rules of the game have changed. The game that exists today will probably be completely different from the game that exists tomorrow. Organizations must be careful not to get locked in to playing by rules that no longer apply, or playing a "game" in a market that has changed or no longer exists.

Mental Model Relay

Makeup of the Team

During the Bcube™ process, it is generally observed that the dynamics of the teams are influenced by the makeup of the teams. When assessing a team's collaborative behavior, it should be noted to what extent its members are homogeneous with respect to their level in the organization, gender, age, race, and so on.

As mentioned previously, in the "Mental Model Relay" exercise, team members are asked to examine an object, write a description of the object, draw, or in some way capture what they feel when they touch the object. This process occurs without talking to the other team members. After each person has had an opportunity to examine and write down descriptions, the group is asked to share individual perceptions and reach consensus as to the identification or description of the objects.

In this exercise, no team member has more information about the objects than any other team member. Every person gets to examine the objects for the same amount of time. The only thing that distinguishes one team member from another is the mental models carried into the Bcube™ exercise. It's like having several witnesses to an automobile accident. Each person, based on individual perceptions, comes away with a different description of what actually happened.

When a group of peers engages in this exercise, it is generally observed that they tend to communicate freely and openly about their observations and perceptions. They are careful not to push their beliefs too forcefully on the rest of the group. They realize that they are each "equal eyewitnesses" to the same set of objects. They seem to understand that at least the mechanics of their experience has been identical. The team members differ only in their mental model perceptions of the objects.

During the consensus-building period, they share their mental models, and compare them with the mental models of their team members. In the discussion that follows, they also test the willingness of their team members to accept new mental models. The team gradually begins to build on members' perceptions, until it has developed a set of collective mental models in the form of descriptions, drawings, or a list of names on which they can all agree.

When the objects are finally revealed, the team recognizes that the consensus list is generally more accurate than the list of any individual team member. This clearly demonstrates experientially the value and power of shared mental models and collaborative team processes. It demonstrates experientially that the team operating as a collaborative whole is greater than the sum of its individual parts.

When the team consists of a group of peers working with a higher-ranking employee, the team members will often wait to see what the higher-level person's perceptions of the objects are before expressing their own. The higher-level person, of course, has no more information or insight about the identification of the objects than do the other team members. However, because the other team members are used to the higher-level person taking charge, it may appear to them that this person is holding back information, being an unwilling participant, or in some cases, failing in his or her role and responsibility as a leader. This can create resentment among the members of the team.

This pattern of behavior was observed with a team and a manager whom we will call Martin. Martin's team members criticized him for not taking a stronger leadership position and a more proactive role during the "Mental Model Relay" exercise. When they were allowed to see the objects, they found that they had only identified three of five correctly.

During the debriefing process, the team members stated that they were waiting for Martin to lead the discussion and express his opinions. They blamed his apparent lack of leadership for their poor performance. They were used to letting him set the pace. Martin was somewhat surprised by their comments. He defended his behavior, stating that he wanted to give others a chance to express their opinions before he spoke up.

What neither Martin nor his group realized, however, was that in their normal work environment one of the factors that distinguishes managers from their direct reports is the knowledge base or experience base that helps shape the manager's decision-making effectiveness. In the "Mental Model Relay" exercise, however, the manager and his team members are all operating from the same level of expertise in mental models. They all have the same general base of knowledge. As a result, when it comes to identifying the objects, no one person's opinion has more weight than that of another.

In this context, opinions are valuable only to the extent that people are able and willing to share and articulate their mental models. This must be done in a way that enlightens and encourages the other team members and helps them reach a team-supported consensus.

In a later exercise, Martin began trying to exhibit the kind of "behavior and leadership" that he thought his group wanted to see. By then, however, the other team members had recognized and learned the power and value of collaborative decision making and problem solving. They had learned just how important their individual inputs were to adding power to the team's ability to solve problems. They were beginning to understand that each person's perspective and individual input was critically important to the success of the whole team. They had become comfortable with these new roles, and they rejected Martin's attempt to exercise what they now saw as unnecessary authority.

In subsequent exercises, Martin learned the value of tapping into the mental models of others as a means of strengthening the collaborative team process. He learned how to blend his skills, observations, and mental models with those of the other team members to achieve more robust problem-solving processes and more resilient solutions.

Everyone Has Something to Contribute

In the "Mental Model Relay" exercise, teams will often have a person who is different from the majority of the team members (female, a member of a different ethnic group, not in the same age group, etc.). It is often observed that when that person has a comment or observation to share, he or she finds it difficult to be heard above the clamor of the other team members.

During the consensus-building phase, this person's input may be partially ignored or may not be acknowledged at all by the other members of the team. Unless the person is especially resilient, he or she may be observed giving up, shutting down communications with the other team members . . . and keeping valuable insights to himself or herself.

When the objects are revealed, team members will often find that they have identified one or two of the objects incorrectly. Many times, the person who had difficulty getting ideas heard by fellow team members will have identified the object or objects correctly. That person takes some pleasure and pride in announcing to the team that he or she had identified the object correctly.

The team, on the other hand, is somewhat shocked, often feeling a bit betrayed. They want to know why the person did not speak up and share this information with the rest of the team for their consideration. The person will generally reply, "I tried to, but you wouldn't listen."

In this experience, the teams learn two valuable lessons:

1. When collaborating, it is absolutely critical to get everyone engaged in addressing the issue. Since God has given us only one brain per person, no brain in an organization can be ignored or wasted. Just because one or two team members seem quiet or don't say very much, that does not mean that they have nothing of value to say.

   Everyone's mental models are valid. Their perception may be just what is needed to unlock the secret of the solution to the problem. The team needs to be sure that each team member has ample opportunity to share mental models with the rest of the team members before critical decisions are made, and before the team moves on to the next point.

2. Team members need to be persistent in finding a way to share ideas. Although this persistence may not be typical of their preferred style of interacting with team members, they realize that when they fail to share their thoughts and insights, they cheat the team. In the end, they may prolong the problem-solving process unnecessarily. In the worst case, they may unintentionally contribute by their silence to the wrong solution.

   When this occurs in business groups, a delay in critical problem-solving processes may mean millions of dollars subtracted from the bottom line. In medical teams, these delays may mean the difference between life and death. Each member of the team is responsible for making sure that his or her input is shared and heard, even if it means pushing in a direction that is different from where the team seems to be headed.

It is important for teams to recognize that even though a team member's specific ideas may be different from the final recommendation, he or she may still provide a critical foundation on which the team can build. It may give the group a mental leg up and be the catalyst for helping the group break through crippling paradigms. It may be just what's needed to open a different access to a new mental model, leading to better solutions.

When Team Members Don't Speak Up

In many teams some members are reluctant to speak up and share their insights and mental models with the team because they are afraid that they will look stupid. They are afraid that their mental models are too far out of the mainstream or too different from those of the rest of the team. Some may believe that the team is so bent on following a certain path that sharing their own mental models, especially if they are thought to be significantly different from those of the group, will make them look, sound, and feel like outsiders. The perceived risk of going against the tide of opinion may far outweigh the perceived benefits of sharing their ideas with the team. They would rather give silent consent than appear different.

It's interesting to note how this behavior might play out in the workplace. In the "Mental Model Relay" exercise there are individuals who are reluctant to share their opinions about a toy in a box. Here the consequences of failing to share their mental model–driven insights are extremely low. If the team does not create an atmosphere where the team members feel comfortable making their mental models and critical inputs available for others to learn from and examine, the team may fail to correctly identify the object.

Suppose, however, that instead of holding back critical information about a toy in a box, the person is reluctant to share true insights about a multimillion-dollar project whose cost is climbing daily. If such reluctance to open sharing is manifested around a game where the stakes are low, how much more prevalent will this kind of behavior be on the job when the stakes are higher? Because the consequences of failure to the team are much greater in the multimillion-dollar project, it is even more important that the team find a way to lower the barriers to communication and create an atmosphere where everyone's input is actively sought, and everyone feels safe enough to offer input for general consideration.

The team must create an atmosphere where each person feels that it is safe enough to risk sharing his or her mental models for the entire team to consider. Like a jeweler examining the many facets of a precious stone, let each team member carefully look at the mental models of their teammates, examine them, and learn from the different perspectives.

If left unattended, the team's failure to lower the barriers to sharing mental models could become a devastating reinforcing loop. Catastrophic events can result when an organization fails to create an atmosphere where its members feel safe enough to openly share their mental models (see Figure 27).

Figure 27
Team Learning Process

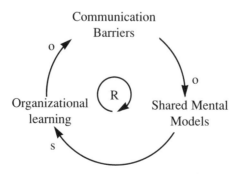

s = change in the same direction
o = change in the opposite direction

The explosion of the space shuttle *Challenger* in 1986 was one such occurrence. It seemed incredible that such a thing could occur. Yet, seventy-three seconds into the launch, the unthinkable happened. The amazing thing was that during the investigation that followed the accident, it became clear that this was an accident that did not have to happen. There was documentation and several memos all written by lower-level people in the Morton Thiokol organization, the designers and builders of the solid rocket boosters, that warned of the possibility of such a catastrophe. These mental models did not get much air time within the organization, however, because these engineers believed that the personal risk of raising a mental model that was significantly different from that of the organization, and perhaps the entire country, was too great. As a result, seven astronauts lost their lives, and the U. S. space program suffered an almost irreparable setback.

A team must understand that it risks potentially serious immediate and long-term consequences if it fails to create a culture where the team members believe it is safe for all the members to share their mental models and learn from the mental models of others.

Interactive Construction

In this collaborative construction exercise an object is disassembled and placed inside Bcube™. Here, the teams begin to examine their concept of vision and leadership.

The participants are not given the identity of the object inside Bcube™. In order to construct the object, the teams must first reach agreement on what the object is. This is accomplished by feel and group discussion. The team must then agree on and articulate the process they will use to put the object together. The vision must be shared by all members of the team. Then they must develop and implement a strategy for putting the structure together.

Developing a Strategy and Leadership Roles

Developing and implementing a strategy usually occurs informally. Often, the team does not realize that a strategy has been developed. Only when asked to describe their building process does it becomes clear to team members that they actually have developed and followed some step-by-step process. Not only have they developed a process for constructing the object, but they have also formed a mental model of what form the team's leadership should take in order to accomplish their objective. For this exercise, a child's ring stacker toy works well.

In some groups, one person assumes the leadership role by grasping the base and requiring the other members to pass the rings to them for assembly. Other groups develop a shared leadership process, where the ring assembly is passed around the box for each team member to add their rings. Some groups form a subteam to assemble the base, while another subteam decides on the relative size and position of the rings. When their individual tasks are completed, they slip the rings on the base.

Since there is no right or wrong way to put the structure together, all of these processes work. The key question each team must decide is, How do we put the structure together, using the competencies that are available to the team? In developing an answer to this question, the teams learn that the task can be accomplished using a variety of team structures. They learn that there is no such thing as a universal team structure. The team structure is driven by the task to be accomplished, the amount of time available, and the individual skills, makeup, and mental models of the members of the team. The team itself is responsible for deciding what structure is best suited for them to accomplish the given objective.

Some groups are at first uncomfortable with what on the surface appears to be a simple concept. This seems to primarily stem from the observation that most teams, especially those in large organizations, are accustomed to having their structure rigidly defined by the organization, with little if any input from the team.

Unfortunately, the driver for structuring and establishing teams in this way tends to be primarily cost-related. While cost is certainly critical, consideration should be given to the people on the team, their skills, and how to quickly get them involved in the decision-making process. When a team structure is imposed, primarily on the basis of cost, it often happens that the team takes longer to accomplish its objectives. This occurs because it takes time for the members of the team to feel like they share ownership of the process. This is common when a structure is imposed on the team, as opposed to a structure that is developed with the involvement of the team.

While cost will always be a critical factor, managers must learn how to balance the cost factor with the human factors, which also impact payback and effectiveness. When cost is the primary driver of team structure, the long-term effect is often a higher overall cost of execution, because of the time that it takes to get the members of the team mentally engaged. This may occur even though the desired impact of the end-product is achieved. It happens because it takes longer for a team, which is not involved early in the decision-making process, to complete its objectives. Because of the longer time it takes to execute the plan, the resulting total cost of the team to the organization may be greater.

When, however, the team is given an early role in deciding the structure and operation of the team, shared ownership and team empowerment are natural outcomes. Effective accomplishment of the objective becomes more than a boardroom goal, driven from the outside. It becomes an extension of the ownership and the empowerment of the team itself.

Bcube™ Is a Practice Field

When Bcube™ is opened, and the completed structures are revealed, the teams often want to put their completed structures on top of Bcube™ to display their success. In some cases, teams are not able to complete the structure successfully. These teams are usually reluctant to display their structures, until they have corrected their mistakes.

In this exercise, participants sometimes impose somewhat of a win–lose significance to the experience. Although the goal of the exercise never focuses on whose structure is correct, whose structure is not, and which team finishes first, there always seems to be some level of embarrassment when a team's construction is not perfect.

While a competitive spirit can help mentally engage the members of the team, it is important to help them understand Bcube™ as a practice field process. In these exercises, it is safe to test the limits of the system. It is safe to make mistakes. As such, there are no winners or losers—only learners.

The Importance of Staying in the Box

It is usually observed that participants in this exercise keep their hands in Bcube™ even after they have passed their rings to the next workstation. This occurs even though they have nothing directly in front of them. Team members generally seem to do this unconsciously. When asked about this, however, the person who puts the final touches on the structure is keenly aware of the presence of the other team members inside Bcube™. They describe a feeling of support and encouragement from the other team members, even though they are not all actively involved in the final stages of the construction.

In a particular workshop, two participants on the same team became frustrated when they were not able to complete or participate in the completion of the task to the extent they desired. In the debrief, they confessed that in response to their frustration, they pulled their hands out of the box. This made the other team members feel that they were not supporting the work, and this caused some resentment.

These two participants were questioned about how they respond to similar frustration in their places of work when they believed their efforts were not being supported by the team. Both these individuals shared that they would typically respond by standing back from the task, becoming less participative. They would gradually shut down their communications, and watch as other members in the department struggled to complete the task. During the debrief, they recognized for the first time that the negative messages they were sending were having an impact on the other members of the team. For the first time, they were recognizing the need to literally and figuratively stay connected inside the box with the other members of the team, both in the workshop and in their day-to-day experiences.

Recognition as a Natural Expression

In the "Interactive Construction" exercise, it is often observed that the groups that are successful at constructing the ring structure will spontaneously recognize themselves for their accomplishment. This is done by applauding themselves, giving high fives, cheering, and so on. As mentioned earlier, being able to spontaneously recognize each other for a job well done represents a significant turning point in the relationship of the team members. Once they cross that self-recognition barrier, the level of trust among team members is greatly increased, along with the positive attitude with which they approach their subsequent exercises.

Many organizations that are trying to implement team-based cultures struggle to find a way to recognize both the teams and individuals on the team who meet or exceed the organization's performance expectations. For many groups, recognition is often a major barrier to implementing an effective team process. To be effective, recognition must be fair. It must be frequent. But, most of all, it must be sincere. One of the few things worse than no recognition is insincere recognition, sometimes called a "plastic stroke." In other words, you are going through the motions, but with little or no attachment to the significant person.

Teams who experience the Bcube™ exercise discover that the most effective recognition is recognition that is generated by the team. This may be because this recognition has its foundation in the team members knowing that they have done a good job. They know that their performance has contributed directly to the bottom-line performance of the organization. Long-term, meaningful recognition will never come from a program that is developed by the organization at large and then imposed on the team.

Team members need to own the recognition process in the same way that they feel ownership for the structure and outcomes of the team itself. In this way, recognition is a natural, sincere response by a team that knows that it has met or exceeded clear objectives. It knows that it has successfully engaged every team member around a shared vision, according to their individual skills and abilities.

This does not in any way negate the value of a corporate recognition program. In this context, however, the corporate recognition program should be an enabler, rather than a driver. It encourages teams to express their mutual appreciation, while avoiding the creation of a corporate framework that is so rigid that it stifles sincerity and spontaneity.

Building New Mental Models

The "Building New Mental Models" exercise is one in which teams and team members are required to openly interact with each other.

In this exercise, the facilitator constructs an object and places it inside Bcube™. The participants are asked to examine the object with their hands, and, using similar materials, construct a duplicate structure on the outside of Bcube™. If there are at least two teams, the participants are allowed to work on their structures for five minutes; then the teams rotate positions, so that they are now working on a structure that another team has started.

Before they begin working on the new structures, however, they are asked to spend ninety seconds talking with the team they are replacing, to learn whatever they can about the new structure before them. They are also asked to spend a portion of that time with the team moving in to replace them at their old structure. They are asked to share whatever information they can that will help the new team assume the task with as little interruption and as much learning as possible.

Building Trust

In a typical workshop, the teams first wrestle with a series of trust issues. The first trust issue usually arises between the team and the facilitator. The team will often wonder if the facilitator is setting them up for failure, either by giving them more pieces than they need to duplicate the structure or by not giving them enough.

As the building process proceeds, the team members continue to build on the high degree of trust they have developed from the previous exercises. When the time comes for rotation, teams, or at least some members of each team, usually express some reluctance about leaving their work and moving on to the next structure. During the debrief, it becomes clear that this reluctance emanates from a lack of trust the teams have for another team's ability to competently take up where they have left off. Each team is so sure that its part of the construction is correct, it is reluctant to have anyone come in and add to or change parts of the structure. In some cases, teams have left "Do Not Touch" notes on the structure, indicating a total lack of trust in the other team's ability to improve on their work.

The incoming team typically resents this, and immediately begins reconstructing the object according to its own mental model of the structure. The incoming teams often openly state during the debrief that they did not like having to come in to "clean up some one else's mess," implying, of course, that the outgoing team did not know what it was doing. As a result of this lack of trust, the teams typically do not take much time to share their critical learning with each other during the ninety-second rotation that would have made their tasks easier. The effect of this behavior is that a high degree of frustration emerges as the structures are alternately built, disassembled, and reconstructed at each rotation.

In some workshops, after a couple of rotations, the exercise has been halted, and the entire workshop group is then led in a discussion about the importance of shared learning and the collaborative functions that occur in high-performance team settings. When the exercise was resumed, the facilitator required the teams to spend ninety seconds sharing their thoughts, insights, and learning with the team that was replacing them at the structure. With the implementation of the collaborative process, the teams became mentally engaged around a common vision. The construction of the objects became a shared objective, as opposed to an individual team task.

Once a level of trust was established among teams, they began to freely share their mutual learning and the structures went up quickly. The structures were generally more accurate than the structures built in workshops where one team worked the entire time on a given structure.

Many participants develop a level of trust where they freely invite other team members and members of other teams to examine and comment on the part of the structure in their own workstation. This is a significant breakthrough. The old paradigms would say that if you invite someone to examine your work, it suggests that you may not know what you're doing, or that you are not competent enough to complete your part of the assignment. But now, under the new team paradigm that begins to emerge, inviting someone to sit at your workstation indicates that the team has successfully created a nonthreatening atmosphere, where the level of trust and value for the mental models and ideas of fellow team members is very high. It indicates a team that is now looking for and recognizing opportunities for shared learning. Team members are experiencing and learning to value a team culture and team behavior, where the whole is indeed greater than the sum of its parts.

Figure 28

In these photographs, it is easy to see the enthusiasm and intensity generated by the "Building New Mental Models" exercise.

Practice Fields and the Core Experience

Even after teams have reached this level of learning and discovery, they still need to reinforce and revisit their core experience on a regular basis. This has the same effect as when family members look through a photo album and relive a memorable vacation, a wedding, or some other significant emotional event they experienced collectively. It helps unite them and galvanize their relationship.

Like pilots in a flight simulator, teams need a way to keep them performing at peak performance after 20,000 hours of working on real-time, real-world problems. High-performance teams have routine drills designed to keep their team skills sharp. It is on the practice field that shared team learning most often occurs. The only teams that tend to have high-risk, low-learning practice fields are those found in corporate organizations. This lack of a practice field breeds conditions where learning deficiencies are common, and employees feel that they are constantly reinventing the wheel.

It is critical that teams keep their new tools sharpened if they are going to be able to use them effectively. They need a way to routinely practice their learning on a practice field where the risks are minimal and the opportunity for learning is high. This is critically important because today's solutions will probably not be adequate to meet tomorrow's challenges. Teams need to constantly develop new capabilities, as a way of increasing their capacity for creating new solutions.

The Bcube™ process can help meet a team's practice field needs. Some Bcube™ exercises take as little as five minutes. Because it is simple and portable and requires very little preparation, Bcube™ can be used in almost any setting as a means of revisiting and galvanizing a team's common experience base as well as sharpening its critical skills.

Bcube™ is also effective as a tool for introducing new team members and getting them involved quickly. Impressions of new team members, like our impressions of people in society in general, are first formed on the basis of external observations: Are they tall or short, male or female, African American or white? Bcube™ encourages a team's value of new members to grow out of their personal interaction, their shared mental models, and the skills they bring to the problem-solving process, with minimal regard to their appearance.

8

The Challenge of Outsourcing

The nature of work and the employee–employer relationship is rapidly changing around the world. It wasn't too long ago that a person who signed a contract of employment with a firm believed that that contract represented a dependable level of financial security for the next twenty-five or thirty years. With the right planning, a person could purchase a modest home, get married, have kids, put them through college, and maybe even save a little without suffering serious financial strain. Retirement was an expected outcome, marked by the traditional gold watch and pension, or some other tangible symbol of accomplishment.

Mutual employee–employer loyalty was the unwritten rule. The average worker did not trouble himself or herself with the rhyme or reason of boardroom decisions. It was believed that as the board dealt with business matters, it could also be trusted to act in the best interests of the employee. Employees believed that pledging their loyalty and hard work was a reasonable exchange for fair and long-term employment in good times and in not-so-good times. Companies behaved like families. Unless an employee did something that was grossly outside the rules, job security could generally be expected.

With the recession of the late 1970s and early 1980s, this picture began to change. The threat of global competitors, gaining access to new technologies and learning how to develop and apply those technologies, grew stronger. Companies in the United States began to take a long, hard look at their internal and external business practices and their ability to remain competitive long term in a global market. Many small operations went out of business during this period. For the first time, many blue chip organizations like IBM, General Motors, and AT&T, which were thought to be invincible business role models for growth, organizational operation, and job security, began using layoffs and head-count reduction through early retirement as a means of reducing costs to improve the bottom line. It became clear that the old paradigms of loyalty and its expected rewards were quickly disappearing.

This description is, of course, a simplification of a very complicated set of events, circumstances, and responses. The general idea here is that the concept of work and the relationship of work to the employer and employee alike has radically changed and will never be the same.

More than ever, organizations are trying to identify their core competencies. What is it that makes them who they are? What is it that gives them identity? What is the blend of technology, skills, and people that gives them that competitive edge? When they find the answers to these questions, they realize that these are the areas in which they want to invest. These are the areas in which organizations want to spend their time and resources. These are the areas they want to nurture, because they represent the core of what gives them their competitive edge.

As a means of reducing operating costs, many organizations are choosing to outsource nonessential functions. This often involves contracting with an agency to administratively manage and hire temporary workers at a lower wage rate to replace higher paid, permanent employees. The permanent employees can then be transferred to areas where more human resources are needed without increasing headcount. When a function is outsourced, the organization also has the option of reducing headcount. This can be accomplished through attrition, or, if more drastic cuts are needed, through layoffs. The organization can then choose to apply its savings directly to the bottom line or to invest in the further development of core functions.

As stated earlier, outsourcing, in theory, is a sound business practice. In practice, however, few organizations actually realize 100 percent of the projected savings. In the April 1, 1996 issue of *Business Week,* the average actual savings from outsourcing are estimated to be about 9 percent, though the identified potential savings typically ranged from 20 percent to 40 percent.[1] In spite of the fact that actual savings often fall far below expectations, outsourcing as a means of streamlining organizations and making their operations more cost-effective is expected to continue. How to outsource the nonessential operations and achieve the savings that are consistent with the identified potential is the challenge of the 1990s and beyond.

Factors in Outsourcing Success

While there are many factors that determine to what extent an organization achieves the projected impact from outsourcing, there are three that apply to this discussion.

The first has to do with information sharing and employees' lack of business literacy. Business literacy is the average employee's level of understanding of what is driving the decisions and actions taken by management. The business literacy of employees also includes an understanding of what they can do to continue to add value to the organization in the changing business environment.

It is the role of management to keep employees informed about the state of the business and the activities of its competitors. It is especially important to keep them informed of conditions and issues that may represent internal and external threats to the success of the organization. When employees are kept informed, it is easier to keep them motivated and positively involved. It is also easier to get general support for management decisions, even when those decisions adversely impact the lives of employees.

This is a very simple principle, but many managers fail to share information because they don't believe that the average employee will understand. Using the techniques described previously in this text, it is possible for managers to understand the mental models of employees. Managers must learn to apply interactive communication skills in sharing information with employees, and use methods that concisely convey their critical messages. They must clearly articulate the challenges ahead and the opportunities that employees may have to make a difference in the outcome.

In today's business world, organizations are primarily geared to provide work, not employment or job security. But organizations still need employees who are committed to quality and cost efficiency. They still need employees who are working to improve performance and increase productivity relative to their customers' needs, wants, and desires. If, however, that kind of commitment was previously given in exchange for job security, then what replaces job security as the motivator for temporary workers and employees?

For the average employee, outsourcing is another name for "threatened job security." When an organization brings in lower-wage-rate, temporary employees to perform the jobs of regular employees who may have given fifteen or twenty years of service, the regular employees may feel betrayed. They have been loyal to the organization's principles and values, but it appears to them that the company is not keeping its end of the agreement. Information that is shared openly, and which answers the 'why' of business decisions as well as the 'what,' is critical if an organization is to receive continued employee support.

The second disconnect in the outsourcing process is the lack of attention given to assimilating temporary employees into an organization. The original employees share a broad, common experience base as it relates to working together in in specific surroundings and in performing specific tasks. The temporary employees, on the other hand, have little or no common experience base.

Even though an organization may have identified a portion of its operation as nonessential, that does not mean that the efficient execution of that operation is not important to that organization's success. In many organizations, once an operation is turned over to the outsourced management group, the new people in that organization get very little routine attention from or contact with employees in the core organization. This continues until customers begin to complain, or unexpected claims have to be paid, or the bottom line fails to reflect the expected impact. Managers often fail to realize that the lack of a common experience base between temporary employees and employees in the core organization can adversely affect the degree to which temporary workers are successful in achieving their performance objectives.

For many temporary workers, an assignment may represent the first time most of them have actually worked together. The group may have gone through some job training, but job training is not adequate to convert a working group into a performing team. If a working group does not have a common experience base, it will be almost impossible for management to consistently forecast with any degree of accuracy the resulting behavior and performance of the group. The degree to which the performance and behavior of a team are predictable and reproducible has its roots in the degree to which the team shares a common experience base. Because these principles are applied so infrequently, it is little wonder that so few outsourcing initiatives actually achieve their projected potential.

As a result, it is not surprising that temporary employees typically go through a long period of development and getting grounded, during which time productivity often sags, the number of errors increase, safety deteriorates, and management begins to wonder whether outsourcing was a good idea after all. The lack of a common experience base is a major, yet often overlooked, disconnect.

There is yet another disconnect that occurs at the interface between temporary workers and the organization. The task is to bridge the gap between the experienced workers who may feel some resentment about the decision to outsource and the temporary workers who are struggling to learn and perform in the new environment. Essential and nonessential functions must fit together like the pieces of a puzzle, because all are important to the success of the organization. There is ultimately only one team, and it is critical that all the members of that team value each other as important to completing the big picture.

These are the kinds of challenges that more and more organizations are facing. The Bcube™ process has been proven to be an effective way of developing a common experience base. There is a growing need to apply this tool in the workplace as the concepts of employer and employee and the practice of outsourcing nonessential operations continue to evolve in today's organizations. If organizations are to be successful in meeting the challenges of their competitors, the changing demographics of their customer base, and doing more with less, it is critical that learning tools like Bcube™ be developed and employed. These tools will prove invaluable in motivating and engaging employees in a safe, nonthreatening learning environment. Where communication barriers can be lowered, a common experience base can be established, and new, dynamic mental models can be constructed.

Conclusion

The ability to operate effectively in a team-based culture is a competency that an increasing number of organizations must develop if they are to remain competitive in the emerging global economy. Doing more with less will continue to be a necessary goal as organizations downsize and look for ways of cutting costs from their operations, while maintaining or improving productivity.

Simple interventions like Bcube™, which can quickly engage teams in gut-level learning experiences, will become valuable development tools. This is especially true for leaders who want to find effective, cost-efficient methods of helping their organizations continue to learn and remain competitive.

Like the gears of a clock, every brain in today's organization must be engaged if that organization is going to be competitive and profitable, and ultimately stay in business. In order for organizations to have a chance at success, every team and every team member must carry out their respective, critical roles. An organization's ability to continually meet this challenge will determine whether it can play to win the game, or just be a player in the game.

Notes

1. "Team" Is a Four-Letter Word
    1. "Workforce 2000," The Hudson Institute, 1987.
2. The Development of a Team
    1. "Reengineering: What Happened?" *Business Week*, January 30, 1995
    2. "Has Outsourcing Gone Too Far?" *Business Week*, April 1, 1996.
    3. Hammer, M., and Champy, J. (1993). *Reengineering the Corporation: A Manifesto for Business Revolution,* New York: Harper Collins.
    4. "Re-engineering Gurus Take Steps to Remodel Their Stalling Vehicles," *Wall Street Journal,* November 26, 1996
3. The Bcube™ Experience
    1. "The Behavioral Ray," Don McMillan and Dave Gordon, APT Consulting, Ann Arbor, Mich.
5. Learning From the Future
    1. "FASTBreak™," David P. Kreutzer, GKA Incorporated, Cambridge, Mass.
7. The Challenge of Outsourcing
    1. "Has Outsourcing Gone Too Far?" *Business Week*, April 1, 1996.

Index*

A
anticipatory learning. *See* learning
Apple Computer, 67, 68
APT Consulting, ix, 26
AT&T, 114

B
barriers. *See* boundaries
Bcube™
    exercises,
        Building New Mental Models, 40, 42, 43, 107–110
        Exploring Mental Models, 40
        Interactive Construction, 102–107
        Mental Model Construction, 41–42
        Mental Model Relay, 40–41, 95–101
        Naming the Game, 40, 90–95
    structure, 22–24
behavioral psychology, 33
bottom line
    employee, 14, 17
    organization, 14, 114, 115
    pressures, 72
    results, 14, *61*, 90, 99, 72, 115

*Numbers in italics refer to figures and tables.

G

General Motors. *See* GM
GKA Inc., v, ix, 51
global economy, 6, 14, *57*, 114, 119
GM (General Motors), 11, 114
Gordon, Dave. *See* APT Consulting

H

Hammer, Michael, 15. *See also* Champy, James
hexagon technique, vi
high-performance teams, 18, 26, 35, 37, 42, 77
    fire-fighters, 78, 80–88 (*see also* CFD)
    Jesus' disciples, 36–37
    Marines, 36
    practice, 53, 54, 77, 85–88
    success factors, 77 (*see also* anticipatory learning)

I

IBM, 11, 67, 68, 114
innovation, 11. *See also* management, motivating employ-
    ees; team

J

job security, 13, *56*, 75, 114, 116. *See also* outsourcing
Jobs, Steven. *See* Apple Computer
Johnson, Bob. *See* GKA Inc.

K

Kennedy, John F., 7
Kreutzer, David. *See* GKA Inc.

L

lay-offs. *See* downsizing
leadership. *See* esprit de corps; management; team

N

O

P